Mughal Land Revenue System

Lanka Sundaram

Qadeem Press

Qadeem Press

Qadeem Press Edition
Breathing Life into Forgotten Pages
www.qadeempress.com

Originally Published by The Basheer Muslim Library in 1929
Reprinted by Qadeem Press in 2025

Find our titles on your favourite online bookstore using the keyword 'Qadeem Press'

PREFACE.

This brochure is the outcome of a paper read before the Historical Association, Noble College, Masulipatam, on the 4th August 1924, and has been reprinted from the *Quarterly Journal of the Mythic Society, Bangalore.*

It is not possible to exaggerate the importance of a study of the Mughal land revenue *system*, if it merits being called a system, as it is the bed-rock on which the present edifice of British taxation in India was built. The writer hopes that this first systematic treatment of the subject will be of use in elucidation of the problems that confronted the importers of this tentative and, to them, foreign scheme and that the work may prove to be a contribution to the history of Indian land revenue in general.

It is with great pleasure that I acknowledge my indebtedness to Professors P. Ratnaiya, M.A., and J. J. Sebastian, M.A., of the Economics and History Departments of Noble College who both encouraged me to attempt this study of one of the aspects of Indian economic history.

My thanks are also due to the joint-editors of the *Quarterly Journal of the Mythic Society*, Bangalore, for kind permission to reproduce the work in its present form under their auspices, and to my friend Mr. Abdul Majid, M.A., for having kindly arranged for its inclusion in the *Basheer Muslim Library Series.*

The writer regrets that owing to the fact that his stay in this country prevented him from reading the proofs, a few mistakes have crept into the text which, he hopes, the reader will not grudge to bear with.

"BRADING",
Cedars Road,
Morden, Surrey.
4th August 1929.

LANKA SUNDARAM.

CONTENTS.

Mughal Land Revenue System.

CHAPTER I.

Introduction.

ONE of the most interesting topics that engages the attention of the student of Indian history and economics is the nature of relationship between the sovereign and the actual tiller of the land in mediæval India. Being at once a subject thoroughly historical and antiquarian, a study of Mughal land revenue system entails the necessary culling of statistics and information from State archives and official returns of the Mughal sovereigns of India, a comprehensive mastery over fact and a laborious assimilation of divergent statements and variant readings. Fortunately for us, Abul-Fazl, the famous vizier of Akbar, bequeathed an invaluable legacy to the student of history in his *Ain-i-Akbari.** But the task of a careful student of this book is not smooth, since he has often to draw a line between sober fact and courtly adulation, interspersed throughout the text.

* The book is mainly concerned with the reign of Akbar. For the later Mughals we have to sound the *Dasturs-ul Amal* or the administrative manuals of Aurangzib which were written in 'the exact antithesis of the style of the *Ain*'. But since the translations of them by Prof. Jadunath Sarkar were not available for me, I was obliged to content myself with the material contained in the admirable article by Mr. Moreland in *The Journal of the Royal Asiatic Society* for January 1922. I have freely made use of Bernier's *Travels in the Mughal Empire*, between the years 1656-88, that is, partly in the reign of Shah Jahan and partly in that of Aurangzib. The translation of *Ain* is the one of Francis Gladwin, as that of Blochmann and Jarret is not accessible to me.

Mughal land revenue system, to do full justice to the subject, is the system of land tenure which was in vogue during the period of Indian history ranging between the years 1526 and 1707, roughly two centuries, between beginning with the accession of Zahirud-Din Muhammad, the famous Babar, and seeing its last phase in the death of the Puritan Emperor in 1707. To pay deference to chronological fact, we have to exclude from our survey the period covered by the years 1542 and 1545 when the Sur dynasty reigned at Delhi, and include the century and a half from the death of Aurangzib to that of Bahadur Shah II, the titular emperor of Delhi,—the period when the degenerated replica of the Mughal empire was left to shift destitute on the billows of the protection afforded by short-lived potentates, until the final inundation of British power which culminated in the momentous exile and death of the last descendant of the dynasty of Timur to which the glorious Akbar traced his pedigree. But the reign of Sher Shah should be reviewed in order fully to understand the revenue system of Akbar whose famous minister Rajah Todar Mal was still a revenue administrator in embryo during his reign and received dexterous training from this emperor himself. The period from the death of Aurangzib may be safely avoided, since during this period the Mughal empire segregated into a congeries of vain dukedoms represented by shallow 'timariots'.

Preliminary Remarks.

According to Manu, revenue consists of a share of the Government in the gross output of the different kinds of grain, taxes on commerce, a small impost on petty traders and shopkeepers, and a forced service of a day in each month by the handicraftsmen. But we are concerned here with land revenue and the various processes of its collection which were in vogue in the Mughal empire. In the preface to his famous work, Abul-Fazl says:* "The assistants of victory, the collectors of revenues and those who are entrusted with the management of the receipts and the disbursements of Government resemble wind; either a heart-rejoicing breeze or a hot pestilential blast." It is evidently clear that much depends on the machinery employed for the collection of the revenues and the spirit in which it works. Custom and principles of equity enjoin upon the king the paramount necessity of being an "upright intendant of finances" in the first place, the discharge of his duties as protector of the husbandmen from oppression by upstarts, the sole fountain of justice and the consequent moulder of the destinies of a nation.

Land revenue depends mainly upon the gross output of the various products of a country which vary in different parts of the land, subject to such determining causes as the vicinity or distance of water for irrigation purposes, the nature of the soil itself which tells upon the nature of the crop, and others. Besides the rate of assessment which varies according to circumstances and the level of administrative vision which a government has attained, the revenue depends upon the extent of the land cultivated and the nature of the crops grown.

India is a country mainly agricultural, and Indian finances always depend largely on the land policy of the

* *Ain-i-Akbari*, p. 11.

Government. A policy intended for the amelioration of the conditions of the people means peace and contentment; a bad and inconsiderate policy means disturbance and discontent. It is too familiar for us that at the present day, while the British Government drew freely upon the various resources of India, nearly 40 per cent of the total revenue is derived from the taxes on land. But in the days gone by, when the taxable resources of the country were found to be few, land revenue came up to 75 per cent or more of the gross receipts of the State.

The annals of the history of the world point out a well-known fact, the perennial struggle between two different schools of thought concerning the attitude of the government towards its subject peasant. The one is to be found in the statement forwarded by Cornwallis in his defence of the permanent revenue settlement: "It is immaterial to Government what individual possesses the land, provided he cultivates it, protects the ryots and pays the public revenue." Here, we should not forget that the "obstinate idealism of Lord Cornwallis", as Dr. Vincent Smith calls it, ignored the fundamental rights of the peasants while turning out to create a system which is all the more worse for them, as expressed in the direct recognition of the zemindar. The other school of thought is to be found crystallized in the memorable statement of Sir Thomas Munro: "We have only to guard the ryots from oppression and they will create the revenue for us." Hence a study of the land revenue system of a country is a necessity if a clear understanding of the significance of a nation's history is desired. Much more so is the case with regard to the

Mughal land revenue policy, since a government though alien to a soil with deep-rooted custom and hoary principles of administration has turned out to evolve a unique type of revenue administration which was borrowed wholesale by the contemporary and later-day Hindu kingdoms in India which were outside the pale of Mughal control, and was groped back to by the early British administrators of India.

Nature of Mughal Land Revenue System.

Mughal administrative system was imported ready-made from outside India. As Prof. Sarkar puts it, "it was the Perso-Arabic system in Indian setting". It is but natural that a succession of sovereigns alive to a sort of settled government in their own native land which lay shrouded in abstract Arabic theory, had had the necessity of giving a sort of orderly government to a country newly conquered, while the conception of chalking out a government of a rough and ready kind to govern the heterogeneous mass of the Hindu community of the age with innate disruptive forces is but a dream. Not to prove derogatory to the Mughal sovereigns, we have to recognize this much, that they were, to some extent, sagacious enough in giving their system a local colouring, in striking a compromise between Hindu traditional customs and prevalent notions of Muhammadan administration.

It may be curious for us to note the chronic antagonism between the tax-payer and the tax-gatherer of the day. But such a condition was warranted by the then prevailing circumstances. It is undoubtedly the fact that the Hindu peasant at the time derived no benefit from the State, on account of the uncertainty of the government, the frequent changes of the dynasties, the unstable nature of the central authority, which were all the more aggravated by internecine warfare and wars of succession. Such a state of things goes to explain the constant struggle between the 'ryot' and the 'sarkar' between the 'never-to-be-extinguished arrears' which the revenue officers were wont to show against the peasant, and the utter disappearance of a *Tabula Rasa* or a clean slate which is to be shown by the peasant.

The prevalence of *Abwabs*, perquisites and presents is another striking note about the Mughal land revenue system. Now, *Abwabs* are illegal cesses current throughout the empire, which will be fully explained elsewhere. The *Ain* mentions that Akbar abolished twenty-nine illegal cesses and vexatious taxes.* At the death of Shah Jahan there were fifty *Abwabs* flourishing. And it is said that Aurangzib abolished about sixty-eight taxes which were against the principles of the *Quran*. Perquisites etymologically mean allowances granted more than the settled wages. But here they are the exactions demanded by the local authorities for their own benefit, and their prevalence indicates the slackening of imperial control over the subordinate provincial authorities. Presents are warranted by long-standing custom and prevalent notions of etiquette. Besides they are a means of getting any favours which people require for their benefit. And this is but a little episode in the drama of social customs inaugurated by the land revenue system of the Mughal emperors.

* *Ain-i-Akbari*, pp. 248-249.

The appearance of intermediaries is another feature to be noted. The services of middlemen are, to a great extent, required for the speedy and efficient collection of the revenue by an alien government from a people naturally reluctant to pay their dues, who have not yet come into an harmonious and beneficent relationship with the government. Akbar recognized the necessity of such men and when conditions required gave them a commission to the extent of 2½ per cent of the State revenues for their labours. This system seemed to be broadly congenial to the government as well as to the people inasmuch as the collection was speedy and effective. But the worst features of the agency of the intermediaries is to be seen when " an occasional Diwan inflated the revenue demand on paper and 'farmed' the revenue to the highest bidder." To this system of farming State revenues by the later Mughals must be ascribed the iniquities of the peasants and the luxurious insolence of the timariots which Bernier lays stress on in his *Travels*.

Another prominent feature to note is the State's sole proprietorship of the lands throughout the empire, a full discussion of which will be presented later on. Bernier's cognizance of and gloomy abhorrence at such a state of things is worth reading. But the State's right over property is a fact widely recognized throughout the other kingdoms of India and quite consonant with the then accumulated wisdom of statecraft which eventually made the peasants lose their respect for private property. Besides, there is no hereditary peerage in Islam. The property which was accumulated by the exertions of an ambitious and diligent nobleman reverted to the State at his death. This amounts to the undoing of life's work at death. A simple illustration may be given. The *Mansab*, say of five thousand, which was conferred on a nobleman by the emperor has no implication of its continuance with regard to his son after the noble's death. Everything is a matter of distinction and imperial favour, while the son of a nobleman may enjoy a greater *Mansab* or none at all. Everything is ephemeral in such a society.

Under the Mughals, the *Sarkar* is the territorial unit while the *Mahal* is a revenue division ; or, to put it in another way, the *Mahal* is the fiscal unit while the *Parganah* is a fixed historical division. All the revenue documents of the Mughal times have, as their avowed objects, the extension of cultivation on the one hand, and the improving of the crops on the other ; but both are so designed as to accelerate the increase of the revenue of the State. Above all, it should be noted that the revenue system need not necessarily be uniform throughout a *Subah* or a province, but was subject to the determining elements of local conditions, and the *Ain* states that " the revenue of a *Bigah* differs in every village ".*

Technique to be met with in the Nomenclature of the System.

Having seen the nature of the Mughal land revenue system, let us now turn to the technique which it has evolved during the period of its vogue. An exhaustive study of the said system reveals a host of unintelligible

* *Ain-i-Akbari*, p. 188.

words which crept into the early British revenue system and which can be seen to some extent even at the present day.

Abwabs :—Illegal cesses and vexatious taxes which were imposed by rapacious and greedy revenue underlings.

Amilguzar :—An officer who shared with the *Fouzdar* the entire administration of a district. His task is in the main the assessment and the collection of revenue. The *Ain* describes him* as a "person who must consider himself as the immediate friend of the husbandman, be diligent in business, a strict observer of truth, being the representative of the magistrate....... He must assist the needy husbandmen with loans of money, and receive payment at distant and convenient periods."

Amil :—A term indifferently used by the *Ain* with the term *Amilguzar*. This much is certain that it is the designation of an executive official under the immediate supervision of the *Subahdar*.

Amin :—"Literally means an umpire, an arbitrator, a trustee for others."† The function of his office is to strike a compromise between the demands of the State and the payments of the individuals. He is under the direct control of the *Amil*.

Balaghat or Highlands, is one of the two administrative divisions effected by Aurangzib in the Deccan. A *Diwan* was placed in its charge with certain executive powers. The illustrious Murshid Kuli Khan worked out

* *Ain-i-Akbari*, p. 261.
† Sarkar : *Mughal Administration*.

a revolution for the better in the existing system of revenue administration there.

Bandobast is a Persian word, the exact translation of which in modern phraseology is the word 'settlement'. "The comprehensive term *Bandobast* or 'settlement' covered all the operations incidental to the assessment of land revenue or government share of the produce."*

Biga or *Jarib* are names synonymously used for measurement as well as a fixed quantity of land. "It consists of three thousand six hundred square Guz."† But the *Ilahi Guz* of Akbar being equivalent to a unit of measurement ranging from 29 to 34 modern inches, the *Biga* may be stated to be the equivalent to a modern half-an-acre and something more.

Bunjer :—It is a kind of land that has been left fallow for five years and upwards.

Buttiey or *Bhaweley* (*Batai*) are systems of realization of revenue in which the State and the peasant divide the grain collected in barns after the harvest according to the stipulated terms of an agreement.‡

Chaudhri :—One of the so-called local authorities—the headman of the *Parganah*. He corresponds in a greater degree to the headman of the village.

Checher :—A kind of land left fallow for three or four years consecutively and then resumed under cultivation.

Dahsala :—The cash rates which are cognizable under the later Mughals acquired the name of *Dahsala*

* Smith : *Oxford History of India.*
† *Ain-i-Akbari*, p. 243.
‡ *Ain-i-Akbari*, p. 262.

for the reason that they were mainly based upon the actual figures for ten years.

Dasturs :—*Parganahs* which followed the same code of revenue administration which are in themselves rare, as the *Ain* points out,* were grouped together for the convenience of administration and a *Dastur-ul Amal* or "customary practice" was given for each group to facilitate smooth government.

Diwan :—Originally the designation of a minister at court, the term was extended to cover the duties of an immediate subordinate of a governor of the province. His office is chiefly one of a fiscal character. Under Akbar, the fiscal and the military powers of provincial authorities were vested in the *Sipahsalar*. But under the later Mughals segregation was made between the functions of the *Subahdar*, purely military, and those of the *Diwan*, purely financial.

Foujdar :—A divisional officer who was appointed to the charge of several *parganahs*.† In conjunction with the *Amilguzar*, he manages the affairs of the district, and answers in a smaller degree to the *Subahdar* of the later times. Besides keeping order, his function is one of facilitating the speedy and the unruffled collection of revenue by the *Amilguzar*.

Challabakhsh :—It is a form of revenue collection, the modern equivalent of which is metayarship. It is the original Indian system where recourse was taken to the actual division of crops.

Ilahi Guz :—It is a unit of measurement which consisted, according to the standardization of Akbar, of

* *Ain-i-Akbari*, p. 188.　　† *Ibid*., p. 257. (Tarrat, II, 40).

forty-one fingers;* its corresponding equivalent in modern measurement varies from twenty-nine to thirty-four inches. The *Ain* traces the *Guz* to Sultan Sikandar Lodi and shows that Sher Shah used a *Guz* of thirty-two fingers for purposes of measurement.

Jagir :—Represents the assignment of lands by the sovereign to persons of distinctive merit and courtly subordinates. The system of granting *Jagirs* has difficulties of its own, but it was prevalent throughout mediæval India.

Alla-ud-din disapproved of the system of payment by *Jagirs*, while under Firuz Shah the grant of such was the rule. Akbar suppressed such grants except rarely for purposes of *Seyurghal*. Later on they were revived. The grant of a *Mansab* had the necessary accompaniment of a *Jagir*.

Kunkut :—The word is derived* from *Kun* which signifies grain and *Kut* to conjecture. In other words, it means estimation of grain by conjecture. "Land is measured with the crops standing" and estimates are made by personal inspection. Revenue experts daily conversant with such a system can calculate with admirable exactitude. In case of doubt, the weighment of the grain derived from a certain plot of land containing good, middling and bad tracts in equal proportions was adopted in order to attain a comparative estimate.†

Karori is the designation given to the actual collector of revenue. The name was originally given to the collector of a stipulated division of land which was estimated to yield a crore of *Dam* (40 Dam=Re. 1) or

* *Ain-i-Akbari*, p. 243.

† *Ibid.*, p. 262.

two and a half rupees. But the term survived in later times irrespective of the amount of revenue collected.

Kheyt Buttiey :—A system of revenue collection in which the State and the peasant divided the field as soon as it was sown.

Lang Buttiey :—Another system of land tenure where the heaped-up grain was divided according to agreement.

Mahal is the fiscal unit into which the whole land was divided by Akbar. According to my computations, the fifteen *Subahs* were divided into 3,367 *Mahals*. It is merely a formal revenue unit, where the revenue was calculated as so much per *bigah*.

Mahsul is the average of produce calculated from equal units of good, middling and bad lands. One-third of the *Mahsul* went as the State revenue under Akbar.

Muqaddam or *Kalantar* are the names given to the local headmen of the villages. Special stress is laid upon them on account of their usefulness to the State in the collection of revenue.

Naqdi :—Presumably a system of revenue collection under which the revenue was paid through the zemindars.

Nasaq :—A system of land tenures quite familiar to the writer of the *Ain*, the general natûre of which is one of contract rather than of a due estimate based on calculations. It was rather an agreement with the zemindars who collected the revenue for the State than a ryotwari system.

Paimaish :—*Zaimaish* and *Zarib* may be taken as synonyms, and they mean the actual measurement of land for ascertaining the extent of cultivation. *Nasq* means the setting aside of *Paimaish* which is the necessary antecedent of the ideal *Zabti* system.

Painghat :—Like *Balaghat*, noticed above, it is the second division of the Deccan which Aurangzib effected for purposes of administration. It is otherwise known as the Lowlands comprising of Khandesh and a half of Berar.

Perowty :—A kind of land which is left out of cultivation for some time so that it might recuperate its deficient mineral constituents by the operation of natural forces upon it, and then resumed under cultivation.

Polej is the ideal sort of land with a rich measure of phosphates and nitrates very much congenial to a good crop and it is never allowed to lie fallow.

Pukhta :—Appointing officers; *Pukhta* means the farming of revenues to certain individuals, naturally to the highest bidders during the process of *Izara* or leasing.

Putteedaree :—"The characteristic of the *putteedaree* tenure is the partition, or apportionment of land in severalty, with joint responsibility. Each owner or shareholder undertakes the management of his separate portion, paying through the headman that proportion of the whole assessment on the estate which, by previous agreement, has been fixed upon this portion of the land."*

Patwari :—"The *Patwari* is employed on the part of the husbandman to keep an account of his receipts and disbursements, and no village is without one of these." He is the accountant-registrar of the village.†

* Robinson, quoted by Cowell. Elphinstone : *History*.
† *Ain-i-Akbari*, p. 249.

Qanungo literally means the 'expounder of the law', or 'customary rules'. As Prof. Sarkar puts it pictorially :* " He is a walking dictionary of prevailing rules and practices and a storehouse of information as to the procedure, land history of the past, etc." Being in possession of ancient documents, some of the *Qanungo* families are veritable mines of trustworthy information. Hence, his designation by the *Ain* as " the protector of the husbandmen " and there is "one in every *parganah*".†

Raqmi :—Mr. Moreland describes it as a system under which " officers wrote down anything they chose, and the record was manipulated in connection with the remuneration of the high officers of the empire ".‡

Ryotwari :—Unlike *Putteedaree* it is a system of land tenure divested of joint responsibility. The individual cultivator was made directly responsible for the payment of the fixed assessment, and it is the most popular and extensive single system of land tenure in British India.

Sarkar is a territorial unit being sub-divided once again into *Mahals*. Several *Sarkars* go to make a *Subah*.

Seyurghal comprises of favours in the form of land which the emperor conferred upon the learned scholars, " the persons who have bid adieu to the world", the needy crippled, and the proud but degenerated noble families who cannot take to any profession on account of their presumed dignity,§ and such other manifestations of religious and large-hearted acts.

* *Mughal Administration.*

† *Ain-i-Akbari*, p. 247.

‡ *Journal of the Royal Asiatic Society*, Jan. 1918, p. 17.

§ *Ain-i-Akbari*, p. 186.

Sipah-Salar :—He is the governor of a province or *Subah* under Akbar with combined powers of the military commander as well as the trustee of the public fisc. Later the functions of the *Sipah-Salar* were segregated, and by the time of Aurangzib, we find the *Subahdar* and the *Diwan* dividing his powers among themselves. He must be vigilant in his business, and cautious in action since he is the guardian of the people and should " keep in view the happiness of the people."*

Subah is an administrative division effected by Akbar for purposes of revenue collection, and it roughly answers to the Presidency of the present day. Originally, there were fifteen such in the time of Akbar but they rose to twenty-one under Aurangzib.

Subahdar is the officer in charge of the *Subah*. He is the supreme military and police authority in the *Subah*, the control of finance being relegated to the *Diwan*.

Taluqdaree is the system of land tenure which was super-imposed over other forms by Muhammadan rulers who had recourse to farming revenues to big officers and powerful chiefs in the State, later developing into hereditary possessions (Yule & Burnell). *Cf.* the famous Talukdars of Oudh.

Taqavvi :—Loans which were granted from the treasury to the poor peasants for the purpose of helping them in the purchase of the plant necessary for agriculture, and realized by instalments at the times of harvest were known as *Taqavvi* loans.

* *Ain-i-Akbari*, p. 253.

Tenab :—A chain of sixty *Guz* in length "composed of bamboos joined together by iron rings"* which was standardized by Akbar for purposes of measurement.

Tepukchy :—An industrious and skilful accountant on whom the *Amil* chiefly depends for trustworthy information.†

Zabti is the ideal form of land tenure which was ryotwar where, after a careful *Zabt* or measurement and consultation with previous accounts, the officers fix the amount due to the State.

Zarib :—As indicated above, *Zarib* and *Paimaish* are synonymous. *Zarib*, though the necessary antecedent of the ideal *abti* system of land tenure, later on turned out to facilitate extortion.

Zemindar is an intermediary who collected the revenue from the cultivator and had a percentage of the collected dues due to the State as his remuneration.

Zemindaree :—"The distinguishing feature of the *Zemindaree* tenure is that when an estate belongs to several proprietors, it is managed in joint stock with no separate possession of portions of land by the sharers."‡

* *Ain-i-Akbari*, p. 243.

† *Ibid.*, p. 266.

‡ Robinson, quoted by Cowell. Elphinstone: *History*.

CHAPTER II.

Akbar's Land Revenue System.

LAND REVENUE SYSTEM BEFORE AKBAR.

There is nothing of Mughal land revenue *system* before Akbar. The ideal form of the original Hindu system of land tenure with a few foreign elements survived till his time. All that was done was that a few greedy sovereigns distorted the original ideal system by engrafting certain undesirable elements upon it. But the basic principles of Manu's Code were never totally lost sight of, nor were they not in any faint degree even recognized.

Under the Sultanate of Delhi true it is that several changes were effected in the system of administration along with the parcelling of the empire under new denominations and consequently the revenue system too underwent a change. Even though the Government's share of produce increased and new taxes were imposed upon the people, their lot was not so appalling like the conditions that prevailed at the break-up of the Mughal empire. Undoubtedly the changes for the worse innovated by Sultans like Firuz Shah Tughlak entailed several hardships upon the people. But instances like this are few. Even a highly centralized autocracy conferred benefits, as the institution of such a system of government meant the removing of the precariousness of security and peace during the mediæval ages notorious for the scrambling for empires, and the people were content. The testimonies of the historian Phiruz Shah (A.D. 1352—1394) and of Nicolo de Conti corroborate the statement. Firuz Shah expatiates upon the happy state of the ryots with a certain degree of prosperity as can be seen in the general use of gold and silver for purposes of ornaments, and from the general goodness of the houses and furniture. Even though he is a panegyrical writer, he does not fail to mention "that every ryot had a good bedstead and a neat garden" which is itself ample testimony to the general comforts of the people. Nicolo de Conti, travelling about the year A.D. 1420 attests to the fact that the state of India was flourishing with beautiful gardens and opulent cities. Ibn Batuta's impressions about the reign of such a cruel and scheming autocrat are nothing but generous, and it is a tribute paid to the satisfactory state of things then prevailing.*

Babar and Humayun did not introduce any changes into the existing nature of things. They were the first conquerors in their dynasty and were mainly occupied with subduing the land and maintaining peace and order. Their time was pre-occupied with suppressing internecine quarrels and open rebellions, and consolidating the empire. So, when we come to the end of the reign of Humayun, we find relief in the benevolent reign of Sher Shah.

Sher Shah is the real inaugurator of Mughal land revenue policy, even though the statement looks technically inaccurate. Sher Khan belonged to the Sur family and rose from the Governorship of Bengal to the Imperial throne of Delhi consequent on the victory gained by him over Humayun in 1542, and for nearly a decade and a half he ruled over the Indian empire from Delhi, when in 1555 Humayun once again regained his lost throne. Even

* See Elphinstone : *History*, pp. 477—478.

though Sher Shah proved to be the best administrator of the Mughal empire before Akbar, he owed much to his predecessors. Alla-ud-Din was his model, and his successes as an administrator of importance are attributable to the latter.

It is no exaggeration when Elphinstone asserts* that Sher Shah undertook measures "as benevolent in their intention, as wise in their conduct". The short period of his reign is replete with the many improvements wrought by him in the administration of the country. His critical judgment was directed mainly at the ascertaining of the exact nature of affairs in the State and the adopting of remedial measures to rectify abuses. He found the coinage had degenerated and reformed it by the issue of an abundance of silver money, excellent both in design and purity. Money is the medium of exchange among the people as well as the means for the realization of State revenue. Bad coinage means the extortion of much money from the peasants when they come up to remit their dues to the State, by the then prevalent process of taking additional bullion to make up the deficiency in weight of the degenerated coins, as we shall see later on. Gresham's Law is sure to operate here and the opulent few will benefit themselves at the expense of the poor and the helpless peasant by the suppressing of the good coinage from circulation and hoarding them up which they alone are capable of. Hence the reform of the coinage is a boon conferred by Sher Shah upon the people of mediæval India, especially in their relationship with the State as regards the payment of their dues

History, p. 447.

where alone they felt the pressure of the drain of their wealth from payment through bad coinage.

Sher Shah did many other things for the benefit of the people. The *Ain* states :*. " Sher Khan or Selim Khan, who abolished the custom of dividing the crops, used this Guz for that purpose." The *Guz* referred to was one of thirty-one fingers in length which consequently falls short of the *Ilahi Guz* of Akbar. From the passage quoted above, it is evidently clear that Sher Shah anticipated Akbar in ways more than one. He made use of a definite unit of measurement ; he abolished crop division and adopted a fixed rate of assessment which is beneficial to the ryot inasmuch as he is in a position to know definitely about his dues to the State ; and made a survey or measurement of all cultivated land. Further, the Rupee of Akbar is traced to him.† Abul Fazl though at times critical in his estimate of Sher Shah's policy does not fail to acknowledge that he was the original of his illustrious master. Had Sher Shah been spared for a longer period, he would have rivalled his successor in fame, and the star of Akbar would have faded before the serene sheen of his halo. But his ill-fated dynasty was given a rude shock by the reconquest of the empire by Humayun in 1555. Whatever the fortunes of the Sur dynasty, it will never fail to be remembered by posterity for having produced Sher Shah.

No sovereign in mediæval India is so prominent as Akbar in the estimation of the student of history. A versatile genius endowed with a rich measure of administrative capacity, Akbar stands out single among

Ain-i-Akbari, p. 243. †*Ain-i-Akbari*, p. 23.

sovereigns, and is famous for his land revenue system. Unlike other emperors of India, he was conscious that he was the father of his subjects, and such a policy as that of Munro that "we have only to guard the ryots from oppression and they will create the revenue for us" was constantly before his mind. Hence is to be expected from him a system of government designed for the welfare of the subjects, and he did actually bequeath one to later sovereigns. Amidst the confusing tumult of mediæval India he made an orderly and beneficial government feasible, and this accounts for his fame and success as a great ruler in the mediæval world.

Akbar's land revenue system for which he is so famous is no innovation, nor is it an invention. His indebtedness to the sovereigns that had gone before him is immense, but this does not in any way diminish the fame of Akbar. He followed the policy of Sher Shah with greater precision and correctness, and then extended it to the various provinces of the country. The best feature of Akbar's policy is its deference to conventions inaugurated by former sovereigns. The *Ain* states in its instructions to the *Amilguzar** as regards the collection of revenue: "Let him see that no *Jizia* be collected, and whatever taxes former monarchs thought proper to remit, do continue to be excused."

The objects of Akbar to eradicate the evils innate in the existing order of things resolve themselves under three heads: correct measurement of the land under cultivation, ascertaining of the produce per *Biga* of land,

* *Ain-i-Akbari*, p. 265.

and the fixation of the state's dues that each *Biga* ought to pay coupled with the rate of commutation in money. The legislation of Akbar as regards the land revenue system was directed towards the realization of these objects.

Besides for political purposes, in order to estimate the exact amount of revenue of the empire, Akbar parcelled his empire into fifteen *Subahs*, one hundred and eighty-seven *Sarkars*, and three thousand three hundred and sixty-seven *Mahals*; or rather, his empire consisted of so many divisions and sub-divisions.* Then, a *Settlement* was ordered to be made and a standardization of units of measurement effected. First, what was known as the *Ilahi Guz* was made a definite unit of measurement. It consisted of forty-one fingers and its modern equivalent varies from twenty-nine to thirty-two inches. Here it is quite informing to note that sovereigns before Akbar, like Sher Shah, used a sort of definite *Guz* for purposes of mensuration and the *Ain* traces the origin of the *Guz* to Sultan Sikandar Lodi.† The standardization of the *Guz* gave a definite unit of measurement, brushed away all kinds of vagueness, about the actual extent of the land, while the great scope for extortion on the part of the officials of the state was thus removed. Akbar also reformed the *Tenab* which is a chain of measurement consisting of sixty *Ilahi Guz*. The *Tenab* which was in use throughout Hindustan before the time of Akbar was made up of rope which left large scope for injustice being done to the ryots since it was subject to variations of length owing to dryness or humidity in

* According to my computation.

† *Ain-i-Akbari*, p. 243.

the atmosphere. Akbar ordered that the *Tenab* be made of pieces of bamboos joined together by iron rings, which guaranteed the integrity of the chain throughout the year. The third change that Akbar effected was the definite measurement given to the *Biga*. It consisted of three thousand six hundred square *Ilahi Guz* and corresponds in modern measurement of something more than half an acre. Several *Bigas* went to make a *Mahal* or *Purganah* and several *Purganahs* which followed the same code were grouped into *Dasturs*. The *Purganah* answers to the lordships of hundred towns in the revenue divisions of Manu.

After obtaining the correct measurement of land, Akbar next turned to the ascertainment of the amount of produce per *Biga* and the state's share in it. For the purpose of making a comparative estimate of the produce of lands, Akbar divided them into four kinds and fixed a different revenue to be paid by each. *Polej* is the ideal and the best sort of land throughout the empire which was cultivated always and was never allowed to lie fallow. *Perowty* is the land that was kept out of cultivation for a short period in order to recoup its lost vigour. *Checher* is a kind of land allowed to lie fallow for three or four years and then resumed under cultivation. *Bunjer* is the worst kind of land that was left out of cultivation for five years or upwards.

Polej and *Perowty* lands were divided for purposes of assessment into three sorts, *viz.*, good, middling and bad. The produce of a *Biga* of each sort of land was collected and the *Mahsul* or the average of the aggregate produce of the three kinds of land was calculated and was deemed as the average produce of a *Biga* of land. The state's share was claimed as one-third of the *Mahsul*. *Perowty* land when cultivated paid the same revenue as the *Polej*. To give an illustration with actual figures* :—

Common Rice.	Best sort of *Polej*.		Middling sort.		Worst sort.		Aggregate produce of the 3 *Bigas*.		*Mahsul*.		*One-third* of the *Mahsul*. *i.e.*, the state's share.	
	Md.	Sr.	Md.	Sr.	Md.	Sr.	Md.	Sr.	Md.	Sr.	Md.	Sr.
	17	0	12	20	9	15	38	35	12	38⅛	4	13

In the case of *Checher* lands which suffered either from rain or from inundations there was a graduation of the state's demand of revenue for a period of five years when it paid equally as the *Polej* land. Nor were *Bunjer* lands totally neglected. An incentive was given to cultivators for their cultivation in the shape of the exceptionally small proportion of the produce taken by the state, coupled with its indulgence in a lenient way of collection which varied with circumstances. Above all, the peasant was given the option of paying either in cash or in kind whichever was profitable or convenient to him. It is worth while for us to remember the difference between the classification of lands made by the British administrators of the present day and that of the Mughal emperors who have gone before them. According to an eminent Civil Servant of the Government of India†: "Modern 'settlement officers' usually

* The figures are those given by the *Ain-i-Akbari*, p. 246.

† Vincent A. Smith : *Akbar*, p. 374.

prefer a classification based on either the natural or the artificial qualities of the soil, and divide the land into classes of clay, loam, irrigated, unirrigated, and so forth. Todar Mal and Akbar took no account of soils, whether natural or artificial, and based their classification on the continuity or the discontinuity of cultivation."

Having ascertained the extent of land under cultivation by means of *Paimaish* or measurement, and having determined the amount of produce per *Biga*, Akbar next proceeded to fix the rate of assessment. Annual returns of revenue were usually made for the different provinces together with the prices prevailing, for the guidance of assessment. And a special collection of prices and revenues was ordered to be made from the sixth to the twenty-fourth regnal years, *i.e.*, from A.D. 1561 to A.D. 1579, both years inclusive. Having found the viziership of Asaf Khan was attended by abuses such as the granting of *Tumkhas* or privileges for collecing revenue on behalf of the state for commission,—"levied partially, according to the particular views of corrupt and self-interested people", as the *Ain* puts it,* Akbar ordered a *Settlement* to be made and entrusted it to the joint management of Todar Mal and Muzaffar Khan Turbati. The empire reaching its greatest limits, the procuring of current prices was found to be attended with difficulties; annual settlements were complained of by the ryots to be exorbitant; and those who had *Tumkhas* were wont to complain of uncollected balances. To avoid inconveniences in collecting prices and settlements of revenues for the previous years, fixing demand-rates annually at

* *Ain*, p. 251.

the headquarters, and to satisfy the people with stating a definite amount of revenue to be paid, Akbar ordered that a *settlement* should be concluded for the past ten years. An aggregate of the rates of revenues from A.D. 1570—1579 was made and the decennial average was fixed as the state demand of revenue. Henceforwards, the collections were made with certainty and the people were satisfied, so goes the statement of the official historian of Akbar's reign.*

Let us now turn to a critical examination of the merits and demerits of the decennial settlement of Akbar. The preparation of current prices and the determining of the rates of collection were, as we have seen above, attended with great difficulties.† The assessment was unquestionably severe since the machinery created to collate the data necessary for fixing the rate and collecting the revenue was to a great extent new, and the *settlement* searching and drastic. Badauni's impressions about the land revenue system of the Mughals may be quoted with profit. Writing of the settlement under consideration, Badauni observes: "In this year‡ an order was promulgated for improving the cultivation of the country and for bettering the condition of the ryots (peasants). All the *Parganas* (fiscal unions) of the country, whether dry or irrigated, in towns or hills, deserts or jungles, by rivers or reservoirs or wells, were to be measured, and every piece of land large enough to produce when cultivated one crore of *Tankas* was to be divided off and placed under the charge of an officer called the *Crori*, selected for his trustworthiness and

* *Ain*, pp. 252-53. † *Ibid.*, p. 251. ‡ A.D. 1574.

without regard to his acquaintance with the revenue officials; so that in three years' time all the uncultivated land might be brought under crops, and the treasury be replenished. The measurement was begun at Fathpur, and one crore was named Adampur, another Sethpur, and so on after prophets and patriarchs. Rules were laid down, but were not properly observed, and much of the land was laid waste through the rapacity of the *Croris*; the peasants' wives and children were sold and dispersed, and everything went to confusion. But he *Croris* were brought to account by Raja Todar Mal and many pious men died from severe beatings, and the torture of rack and pincers. Indeed so many died after long imprisonment that the executioner or headman was forestalled" [Badauni ii, 189]. This passage clearly brings out the truth of the statement that measures wise in their design often prove to be troublesome at the time of their inauguration and leave much room for abuses to creep into the system, since the peasants will not be in a position to comprehend their true nature, while greedy and rapacious officers exact much from them with impunity. Yet the system worked very well after a time when the peasants were accustomed to it as will be evident from the annals of later times.

The prolongation of the term of *settlement* mitigated an inherent evil in the system. Annual settlements mean uncertainty of the assessment to be paid by the peasant to the state which varied according to the nature and yield of produce year after year. This makes the peasant indisposed to cultivate richer lands since even [illegible] he receives a much greater yield by the cultivation of such land, he has to pay an increasingly greater amount of tax to the state. Thus the labours of the peasant for the better cultivation of the land will not be fully rewarded. Whereas, on account of the decennial settlement, Akbar fixed the amount due from the peasant to the Imperial Treasury, while the peasant was given the hope of enjoying a greater profit in case he extended and improved his cultivation.

We may now turn to the Government's share of produce under Akbar. Akbar took one-third of the *Mahsul* as indicated above. But the ideal rate of assessment in the Hindu period of Indian History is only one-sixth. Akbar was not unconscious of the excessive demands he was making when he demanded one-third of the produce as the rate of assessment. He reduced the *Jehat* or duties on manufactures to the extent of five per cent.* Even though the share of Government in the produce of the land was only one-sixth under Hindu sovereigns, there were several vexatious taxes, known as *quitrent* prevailing. The *Ain*† mentions that twenty-nine taxes were abolished by Akbar in order to give compensation to the peasant for the greater proportion of revenue demanded by the state. There is no direct evidence whether Akbar's orders for the abolishing of those cesses were carried out to the fullest extent. But this much is certain that the payment of the revenues was lenient, and remissions many. The instructions to the *Amilguzar* provide for a lenient way of the collection of revenue: "Let him agree with the husbandman to bring his rents himself at stated

* *Ani-i-Akbari*, p. 247. † *Ibid.*, pp. 248-49.

periods, that there may be no plea for employing intermediate mercenaries."* Besides, there is direct testimony that the system was lenient. "The husbandman has his choice to pay revenue either in ready money, or by *Kunkut* (estimation of crop while it is standing) or by *Behawely* (division of produce collected after the harvest into barns)."† Again the *Ain*‡ states that in the case of Bengal the peasants "pay their annual rents in eight months by instalments" and bring the revenues themselves to the Treasury. Dr. Vincent A. Smith doubts§ the extent to which remissions were granted. But there is evidence enough that remissions were usually granted when occasions demanded them. The Sikh tradition points out that Akbar remitted the land revenue of the Punjab at the intercession of Guru Arjun during the famine year 1595-96. There is the direct evidence of the *Ain* that the remission of taxes like the *Baj* and *Tungha* as regards Cashmir reduced the revenues to some extent. I quote the passage of the *Ain*:|| "His Majesty granted a general remission of all *Baj* and *Tungha*, which deductions amounted to 67,824¼ *Kherwars*, or 898,400 *Dams*; and for the further ease of the husbandman, the *Kherwar* was increased in value by five *Dams*." From this it is evident that twenty-two thousand four hundred and sixty rupees, tolerably big a sum for a single *Suba*, was remitted in the case of a single province as Cashmir; and further, enhancing the exchange value of a *Kherwar* by five *Dams* ns a proportionate loss to the state

* *Ain.*, p. 264.

† *Ibid*, p. 251.

‡ *Ibid.*, p. 302.

|| P. 442.

while being a definite asset and advantage to the cultivator. This is enough evidence to assure us that remissions were granted when occasions required them. Incidentally, it can be seen that the currency policy of the Mughal empire played a material part in the relationship of the peasant to the state, and we will come to this later on.

As Wilton Oldham observes "Akbar's revenue system was ryotwaree" where "the actual cultivators of the soil were the persons responsible for the annual payment of the fixed revenue," and there is the direct evidence of the *Ain* that the *Amilguzar* must "not entrust the principal men of the village with making the estimate of *Kunkut*,......but......transact his business with *each* husbandman *separately*,"* and hence there is no farming of any branch of revenue. Another feature about Akbar's land policy is the gradual resumption of *Jagirs* into *Khalsa* or crown-lands as far as possible, and the payments of salaries were made in money only. Dr. Vincent Smith says that Akbar never recognized the Zemindar, but the statement is subject to qualification. No doubt Akbar tried to avoid the Zemindar as far as possible. The instructions to the Foujdar require of him a vigilant watch against the Zemindars and other confederations.† Besides there are thirteen Zemindars mentioned in the *Suba* of Berar‡ and in the case of Multan the "Zemindar takes from the merchant a duty of 10 *Dams* upon every man's load, and he also pays to the state a rupee for every eighteen maunds of salt that he transports."|| Besides Akbar allowed grants of

* *Ain.*, p. 263. (Italics mine.) † *Ibid.*, p. 257. ‡ *Ibid.*, pp. 346-49.
|| *Ain-i-Akbari*, p. 397.

land for purposes of *Seyurghal.** Hence we may conclude that the *Zemindar* was prevalent in the time of Akbar, only occasionally in the outlying *Subas*, and that, unlike the extortionate powers enjoyed by the later *Zemindars*, these were not totally absolute under him. At least, it may definitely be assumed that the idea of *Zemindari* tenure is under a specific discount.

Raja Todar Mal.

Among the courtiers that surrounded the person of Akbar no name is better remembered than that of Raja Todar Mal. Abul Fazl may have been the greatest genius of the time; Shaik Faizi may have been a poet of the first magnitude; Tansen may have been the best musician available; Raja Birbal may have been the most intimate friend by the side of Akbar; Raja Man Singh may have been the best warrior to count among a host of others; but Raja Todar Mal is most prominent in this list as a genius endowed with the skill of a benevolent statesman and a cautious revenue administrator.

Raja Todar Mal served under Feroz Shah, as has already been pointed out, and gained his first experiences as a revenue administrator under his ægis. Having entered the service of Akbar he was favoured with the grant of a *Mansab* of four thousand,† and thenceforward he put all his administrative capacities at the disposal of Akbar. But for him we may reasonably say it would have been difficult, if not impossible, for Akbar to hand down to posterity such a system of Revenue Administration as the one that he actually evolved.

* *Ain-i-Akbari.*, p. 186. † *Ibid.*, p. 164.

The character of a person always colours his actions. More true is it in the case of a revenue expert like Todar Mal, and on account of this his policy takes altogether a different shape from the one which he actually gave it. In his *Akbarnamah* Abul Fazl "describes him as entirely devoid of avarice and quite sincere, but of a malicious and vindictive temper,"* and the latter half of this quotation is corroborated by the statement of Badauni which has been just cited. Hence, the harshness of his system though benevolent in nature.†

The constructive revenue system of Todar Mal has two aims in its view: the increase of revenue ostensibly, of course, not by extortion but by the increase of cultivation and the security of the peasant. The desires of that famous finance minister were given the opportunity of being translated into concrete measures when he was first appointed Governor of Gujarat in 1574. Here he effected some of his first reforms. He restored to local jurisdiction some of the districts which had been recently conquered; a systematic measurement of land was made as a preliminary to settlement; the assessment was determined with reference to the area cultivated and the nature of the crop grown; and in certain provinces the Government realized their dues either by *Kheyt Buttiey* or by *Lang Buttiey*, *i.e.*, either by the division of fields between the Government and the agriculturists while the crops are standing or by actual division of heaped-up corn. But it is certain

* *Cf.* Elphinstone: *History*, p. 531.

† *Cf. Ain-i-Akbari*, p. 26—"His Obstinate Despotism."

that the revenue of the state was to some extent reduced.

Todar Mal anticipated his later settlement while he was introducing reforms in Gujarat. He was given the necessary opportunity for the working out of his reforms on a large scale when he was appointed vazier in conjunction with Muzaffar Khan Turbati in the fifteenth regnal year, *i.e.*, in 1570. Ten imperial *Qanungos* were appointed to collect the accounts of the provincial *Qanungos* and a new *Zumma* was formed in contradistinction to the corrupt one in vogue under Asaf Khan, the preceding vazier, * at the headquarters. Vincent Smith says,† "the amount of demand was somewhat less than in former years, but the discrepancy between the estimates and the actual receipts was diminished." The later part of his statement is subject to qualification. The *Ain* says, ‡ "this settlement is somewhat less than the former one (*i.e.*, of Asaf Khan); however, there had hitherto been *a wide difference* between the settlements and the receipts." The reason for this is not far to seek; and the passage quoted from Badauni elucidates the doubt. The searching nature of the system might have resulted in the desertion of land by the ryots, while several abuses might have crept into the system at the time of its inception. Later on, there is no room for doubting, the system worked fairly well. The statement that the system worked fairly well is corroborated by the fact that the system was adopted by Ibrahim Adil Shah II of Bijapur a

* *Ain*, p. 251.
† *Akbar the Great Mogul*, p. 370.
[illegible] 252

contemporary of Todar Mal. The testimony of Meadows Taylor who has had enough local knowledge may be quoted : "The land settlements of the provinces of his kingdom, many of which are still extant among the district records, show an admirable and efficient system of registration of property and its valuation. In this respect the system of Todar Mal introduced by the Emperor Akbar seems to have been followed with the necessary local modifications."*

New Official Machinery.

We may now turn to the officialdom which Akbar created in his bureaucratic system of government designed for revenue purposes. *Sipah-Salar* is the supreme head of military and revenue affairs of a *Suba*. As the *Ain* puts it,† "he must constantly keep in view the happiness of the people, and never suffer himself to be negligent in business..............Considering his office to be that of a guardian, let him act with utmost caution." Whatever may have been the real state of affairs, the minute attention of Akbar for the people's welfare is clear from this passage. Next to the *Sipah-Salar* come the *Faujdar* and the *Amilguzar* who manage the military and revenue affairs of a district respectively.

It is curious and informing to note the order in which the *Ain* enumerates the officers and their duties. First there is the *Sipah-Salar*, and next to him come the *Faujdar*, the *Kotwal*, the *Amilguzar*, the *Tepukchi*, and the *Treasurer*. From the order of arrangement it

* Meadows Taylor as quoted by Smith : *Oxford History of India*, p. 296.

† *Ain-i-Akbari*, p. 253.

is clear that importance was given first to the military and police officers inasmuch as their assistance was necessary for the latter three revenue officials pure and simple in the discharge of their duties.

Now, *Faujdar* is a divisional officer who was appointed to the charge of several *parganas.* He asisted the *Amilguzar* in the collection of the revenue and was to quash the confederations of rebellious zemindars. *Amilguzar* is an officer whose purpose is mainly the assessment and collection of revenue. The idealistic description of him by the *Ain** is really deserving since he is the person who had supreme control over the peasant, and could be either extortionate or lenient.

Next to the *Faujdar* and *Amilguzar* come the *Putwari*, the *Qanungo*, the *Amin* and the *Karori.* "The *Putwari* is employed on the part of the husbandman to keep an account of his receipts and disbursements, and no village is without one of these."† The *Qanungo* literally means "expounder of law" or "customary rules". He is styled by the *Ain* as the "protector of the husbandman".‡ Being in possession of ancient documents some of the *Qanungo* families are veritable sources of trustworthy information. The *Amin* means "an umpire, an arbitrator or a trustee for others."§ He is chiefly concerned with the striking of a compromise between the exorbitant demands of the state and the evasive replies of the husbandman. He is under the

* P. 261.

† *Ain*, p. 247.

‡ *Ibid.*

§ Jadunath Sarkar: *Mughal Administration* (Patna University Readership Lectures).

direct control of the *Amil.* The *Karori* or *Krori* is the actual collector of revenue. It is one of the peculiar words introduced into the nomenclature of state-craft by Akbar, and stood for the collector of a crore of *Dam* or two and a half lakhs of rupees. But later on the term was applied to collectors of revenue irrespective of the amount of revenue collected. It may be interesting to note that Akbar granted the *Suddu-i-Putwari* or two per cent for the *Putwari*),* and that this commission was divided equally between the *Putwari* and the *Quanngo,* besides their actual salaries which ranged between rupees twenty and fifty according to their rank. Next in order comes the *Tepukchi,* an industrious and skilful accountant, on whom the *Amil* chiefly depends for trustworthy information. His duty is to despatch daily returns of the receipts and balances of every village to the *Amil* and keep the latter informed about any sudden calamity that might befall a village. Lastly comes the *Treasurer,* and the Treasury was kept at the residence of the principal officer in the district. A strict watch was kept over the treasury and the treasurer was ordered to accept the coins of former reigns which possessed the necessary weight as bullion, while disbursements were to be made with the express approbation of the *Diwan.*

A salient fact for us to note is the attempt on the part of Akbar to gain thoroughness in matters of revenue collection. The daily returns of the *Tepukchi,*† the weekly returns of the *Amilguzar*‡ and the counter-signature

* *Ain-i-Akbari,* p. 247.
† *Ibid.,* p. 267.
‡ *Ibid.,* p. 264.

of the *Amil* on the memorandum of the *Treasurer** go to support the statement.

We may now turn to the different means of realizing the state's proportion of the produce and those systems legalized by Akbar. We may broadly divide the various systems of revenue collection into three heads: the *Ghallabakhsh*, the *Zabti* and the *Nasaq* systems. Let us now consider the nature of the separate systems and their merits and demerits.

The *Ghallabakhsh* is the original Indian system where an actual division of crop was made between the cultivator and the state. Its equivalent in modern phraseology is meteyarship. This process of realizing the state's proportion of produce is sub-divided by the *Ain* into four kinds.† They are: the *Kunkut* or estimation of crop by conjecture; the *Buttiey* or the *Bhaweley* where the grain heaped up in barns after the harvest was divided according to agreement; the *Kheyt Buttiey* where an actual division of land was effected as soon as the field was sown; and the *Lang Buttiey* where the produce collected into heaps was proportionately divided. The first two methods are liable to imposition. But this system of crop division is subject to many difficulties. The revenue under such a system will be vacillating on account of its dependence upon the seasons, the accuracy of the officials, and the area of land sown and the yield per unit. But it is evident from the *Ain* that it was prevalent to some extent under Akbar. It was to be seen in Cashmir where the text reads:‡ "the crops shall be equally divided between the husbandman and the state"; in Tatta where the "husbandman divides his crops with the government"*; besides many other places. Crop division was also resorted to in case of *Bunjer* lands.† It may also be noted here that commutation in money was permitted when the peasant desired. It may here be observed that this ancient Hindu mode of realizing state revenue given wider currency to by the Mughals was in part resorted to by the East India Company during the eighteenth and the nineteenth centuries.

The *Zabti* system is the alternate system chiefly used by Akbar in order to eliminate the uncertainties and difficulties inherent in the system of crop-division. It is an equitable, though not lenient, system of revenue collection. Its chief characteristic is the fixed rate of assessment determined according to the nature of crop and the payments of assessment in previous years. It gave definiteness to the state's dues from a cultivator, while to the latter it gave ease and scope for improvement. It is otherwise known as the *Regulation System*. The "questionable statements regarding the *Zabti* system" as enumerated by Mr. Moreland‡ are the term of the settlement, the distinction between grain-paying and cash-paying crops, and the post of *Karori*. They are too controversial but the possible facts are that a decennial settlement was made by Akbar,§ that there was a distinction between grain-paying and cash-paying crops|| and that the post of the *Karori*, which was treated

* *Ain-i-Akbari*, p. 402. † *Ibid*., p. 250.

‡ *Journal of the Royal Asiatic Society*, January 1918, pp. 25-27.

§ *Cf*. *Ain*., p. 252.

|| *Cf*. *Ibid*., p. 246, where turmeric, cucumber, hemp, and other crops were "ordered to be paid in money".

as an integral part of Akbar's revenue system, disappeared very quickly, as is evident from their not being mentioned by the *Ain* and the miserable lot of the *Karoris* as is apparent from the description of Badauni might have resulted in the general abhorrence of the people of that post.

Nasaq or summary assessment is the third and last kind of revenue collection. It is a system quite familiar to the writer of the *Ain* where he makes direct mention of it as regards the revenue collection of Bengal* and Guzarat† besides several other places. That it was not an innovation of Akbar is beyond all doubt since an Emperor who is mainly interested in the welfare of the people could not have resorted to such a sort of assessment; and if it was prevalent to some extent under his *régime* it was only due to considerations of expediency, since many parts of his empire being newly conquered were unruly and troublesome. For example, Bengal always proved to be a scorpion in the side of the Mughal emperors, while Guzarat was recently conquered. The essential nature of the *Nasaq* system is one of contract and hence odious to the *Zabti* system with its necessary antecedents of *Paimaish* or measurement of land, and equitable assessment. It is an agreement rather than a detailed assessment, a Zemindari rather than a ryotwari system, a mutual contract rather than a detailed examination of the yield of crop. It is a common and convenient method of assessment and was at times resorted to on account of it being a simpler and cheaper mode of

* *Ain-i-Akbari* p. 302.
† *Ibid.*, p. 350.

revenue collection than the *Zabti* system, especially in newly conquered *Subas*.

Administration of Individual Subas.

We may now pause for a moment and consider the general nature of revenue collection under Akbar. Even though he tolerated crop-division and the *Nasaq* system of assessment, the ideal and usual form was the *Zabti* system based on an actual measurement of land, the nature of the crop grown and the equitable rate of assessment. A consideration of the forms of revenue collection in the various *Subas* elucidates the statement. I now proceed to describe the modes of collection in the fifteen *Subas* of Akbar.*

Agra :—The *Zabti* system of assessment was largely in vogue with slight exceptions as in the case of *Seyurghal* revenue. The *Ain* states that eleven *Sarkars* out of thirteen pay revenue in the case of the lands granted for purposes of *Seyurghal*. For the *Mahal* of Baground no figures were given.

Ajmir :—It was not assessed uniformly. *Ain* states "The revenue is in general a seventh or an eighth of the produce of the harvest, little being paid in ready money" (pp. 367-68). Of the seven *Sarkars* comprising the *Suba* areas were not given for Jodhpur and Sirohi, while in *Sarkar* Bikaner all the eleven *Mahals* were left blank while a round sum was given as the revenue of the *parganas*. From this it is evident that to some extent either the Zemindari or the *Nasaq* form of revenue

* The page numbers are those of the *Ain*.

collection was prevalent. Four out of seven *Sarkars* paid *Seyurghal.*

Allahabad:—Mostly the *Zabti* system. But the whole of *Sarkar* Bhathkhra with its thirty-nine *Mahals* are not given any figures, neither are there given the names of the *Mahals.* Besides seven *Mahals* were omitted, while two *Mahals* were grouped in one case. Hence it is evident that the *Naqdi* system existed and the revenue was paid through Zemindars. Nine provinces out of ten paid *Seyurghal.*

Behar:—The *Zabti* system is generally prevalent. " It is not customary in Behar to divide the crops. The husbandman brings the rents himself " (p. 317). One *Mahal* is missing in the *Sarkar* of Behar while the *Sarkar* Monghyr was not given any measurement. Anyhow the *Ain* mentions " unmeasured land consisting of sixty-one *parganas* " (p. 319); while one *Sarkar* (Behar) out of seven mentions revenue from *Seyurghal.* From this it is probable that some form or other of *Naqdi* system was prevalent in the *Suba.*

Bengal:—The prevailing system was *Nasaq.* The *Ain* says " it not being customary in this *Suba* for husbandman and the Government to divide the crop...... the produce of the land was determined by *Nasaq* " (p. 302). A peculiar feature to note about the *Suba* of Bengal is that its *Tukseem Jumma* does not mention the area of even a single *Sarkar*, Jennetabad were not given any figures, while the *Mahals* of the entire *Sarkars* of Kullengdundpaut and Raje Mahendreh (Rajahmundry ?) were not enumerated. Another point which supports the statement that *Nasaq* was prevalent here universally is that no mention of *Seyurghal* is made as it is characteristic of the cases of *Subas* where the *Zabti* system was prevalent.

Berar :—In general *Nasdq* and the *Ain* makes mention of thirteen Zemindars besides, perhaps, many others (pp. 346-49). Besides, Manikdrug is an independent territory (p. 348). Eight *parganas* in *Sarkar* Kullern passed into the hands of an independent Zemindar, while twenty-two *parganas* in *Sarkar* Kherla were independent under Zemindars (p. 349). Eleven *Mahals* are missing while eighteen *Mahals* give blank returns. Four out of. seven *Sarkars* pay *Seyurghal*. No extent of land is given.

Delhi :—Prevailingly *Zabti*, but there are traces of the Zemindari form of land tenure. For example, *Sarkar* Reytwari gives no aggregate revenue statement while *Sarkar* Kumaun, evidently a hilly tract, omits the returns for five *Mahals* and remarks "no account is made of the other five *parganas*" (p. 529). The same *Sarkar* does not mention its area. Seven out of eight *Sarkars* pay *Seyurghal*.

Guzarat :—Being not homogeneous, several forms of revenue collection were prevalent. But the *Ain* assures us that *Nasaq* was prevalent for the most part, and that *Paimaish* was seldom resorted to. Here it should be noted that Surat paid by estimate (p. 368). Two *Mahals* are missing while two more were not mentioned in *Sarkar* Surat. The *Mahal* Dhamnud in *Sarkar* Kodehra gives no returns. A peculiar feature about *Sarkar* Surat is that port duties were not paid in the usual *Dam* but in *Mahmudi*. Seven out of nine *Sarkars* mention *Seyurghal*.

Kabur :—Mainly crop-division. The various systems were given only for *Sarkars* Cashmir, Kandahar and Kabul. In Cashmir crop-division by estimate was prevalent, it being not customary to have recourse to measurement or to receive money (p. 422). Crops were equally divided between the state and the peasants. In Kandahar, "most kinds of grain were computed in *Kherwars*", the *Kherwar* being an equivalent to forty Kandahari or ten Hindustani maunds. From the description of the revenue system prevalent in Kandahar it is evident that the demand of the state is abnormally high as compared with other provinces of Akbar. Though theoretically one-third marked the state's portion of the yield, two-thirds was demanded usually from the total produce of the land. The *Tukseem Jumma* of the *Suba* of Kabul does not mention the areas for any of the *Sarkars*, while as regards some *Sarkars* no amount of revenue was known as due. The *Sarkar* Kabul contains a certain amount of *Seyurghal* land while *Sarkar* Puckely does not mention the amount of revenue and the *Mahals* comprising it. As regards *Sarkars* Puckely, Swat, Deruneyun and Issakhyl they were expressly stated as hill tracts inhabited by unruly tribes. Hence the occupation of Imperial Government in those *Sarkars* was mainly military. Again in Kandahar there is a distinction between cereals and other crops, and the revenue was collected either by measurement or by contract (pp. 447-48).

Khandesh :—The *Ain* styles it as Dandes. No definite system of revenue collection is mentioned but the old system, which is obscure, might have been followed. A curious point to note is the payment of revenue in *Berary Tungahs* and this also shows that an old system was still pursued under Akbar. The *Berary Tungah* is equal to twenty-four *Dams*, and hence two *Tungahs* roughly go to make an *Ilahi Rüpee*. The *Suba* of Khandesh was comprised of thirty-two *Mahals* out of which three were not mentioned, while their revenues were stated. The measurement of the *Suba* was not given.

Lahore :—Mostly *Zabti*. The Zemindar collects revenue from the merchant and pays a transport duty himself to the state (p. 397). Five *Mahals* are missing, while no returns were given to *Mahal* Jeffroth in *Sarkar* Retchnabad. Three "separate *parganas*" are mentioned without the extent of their areas. A point to note here is that the *Suba* was divided into *Duabehs* evidently the doabs between the five rivers. All the *Sarkar Duabehs* except the "separate *parganas*" mention *Seyurghal*.

Malwa :—The *Zabti* system was the rule. Anyhow the *Ain* mentions "the husbandmen here pay the revenues in gold mohurs and elephants" (p. 331), by which we hazard the suggestion that cash rates were prevalent. Ten *Mahals* are missing. Measurement was not given to three *Sarkars* while the aggregate revenues were not stated for two *Sarkars*. *Seyurghal* is mentioned in the case of eight *Sarkars* out of twelve.

Multan :—The system prevalent in this *Suba* was *Zabti*. One *Mahal* is missing. The *Suba* consists of eight *Duabehs*, two *Sarkars*, and two other divisions stated as "separate *parganas*". *Sarkars* Multan and

Deybalpur do not enumerate their constituent *Mahals*. All the divisions of this *Suba* mention the revenue of *Seyurghal*.

Oudh :—This *Suba* consists of five *Sarkars* and the system prevalent was *Zabti*. Three *Mahals* are missing. All the *Sarkars* mention *Seyurghal*.

Tatta:—Prevailingly *Ghallabakhsh*, the system was described as one where "the husbandman divides his crops with Government, and is allowed to keep two-thirds" (p. 402). As is implied in the system of crop-division no area of the *Suba* and the various *Sarkars* is stated, since the system has nothing to do with measurement of lands. Two *Mahals* are missing while *Seyurghal* is not mentioned.

How the Tukseem Jumma was compiled.

Having examined in detail the various systems of land tenure prevalent in the different *Subas*, together with the peculiar features of each, we may now pause for a moment and analyse the principles according to which the *Tukseem Jumma* was compiled. A comprehensive understanding of those principles alone makes us assimilate the dumb figures and multitudinous statements relating to revenue returns that abound to a great extent in the *Ain*. The returns which indicate the yield of revenue from *Seyurghal* suggest that grants of land to individuals were prevalent in those areas. The state's revenue represented by round numbers suggests, presumably, that the zemindari form of land tenure was prevalent in those locations since absolute round figures cannot come out of a careful survey and an equitable rate of assessment with each individual.

Statistics mentioning no extent of land may be taken as denoting the prevalence of crop-division since it has nothing to do with measurement but mainly depends upon the actual yield of crop; or may suggest the prevalence of *Nasaq* or summary assessment. In cases where no figures were given representing the amount of revenue due to the state, and no extent of territory mentioned, we may conclude the prevalence of the *Naqdi* form of collection of revenue. And where the extent of the land and the amount of the revenue were given, and the enumeration of the *Mahals* was complete —of course leaving a fair margin for cases where actual returns were difficult to get, we may name the prevailing system as *Zabti.**

Summary.

To conclude the survey of Akbar's land revenue policy we may note the revenue of the state during his reign. Abul Fazl states it as "640 *Krors* of *Muraditankas*" or ten crores of rupees (64 *Muraditankas*=Re. 1), while Nizam-ud-din Ahammad, another fiscal authority, states the revenues were something less than ten crores of rupees.† When compared with the revenues of the later Mughals, especially under Aurangzib, when the highest water-mark of state revenues, thirty-eight and a half crores of rupees, was reached in 1697, we may conclude that Akbar's revenue was very small.

Under Akbar, the ideal form of revenue collection was the *Zabti* system. It was essentially ryotwar, and gave definiteness to the state's demands while securing

* These are the results which my researches have produced.

† See Mr. Keene's paper in the *Journal of the Royal Asiatic Society*, 1887, p. 498.

ease to the peasant. This system was pushed as far as it was possible, of course, modulated according to the needs of local conditions. The prevalence of *Nasaq* may be explained as a make-shift system of revenue collection in newly-conquered and rebellious provinces such as Khandesh, Kabul, Tatta, Bengal and Behar. The resumption of *Jagirs* into *Khalsa* was thorough to the extent that it was advisable and practicable. The zemindars though existing in Akbar's days were not absolute like those prevailing under the later Mughals but were merely people given a commission on state revenues for their effectual collection. The system was lenient beyond all doubt, and the peasant had the choice of paying either in cash or in kind as he thought convenient and profitable to himself. An attempt at perfection of the bureaucratic machinery was made and was to a great extent attended with success. Remissions were generally granted when unforeseen calamities befell a province, while several vexatious taxes on manufactures and other trading concerns were abolished or reduced; and the *Ain* states that twenty-nine taxes were declared illegal and abolished. Whatever may have been the effect of the orders of Akbar, whether they were fully carried out in practice or not, the fact remains that the lot of the peasant under Akbar was more happy than under the later Mughals.

CHAPTER III.

Under the Later Mughals.

PARTIAL SURVIVAL OF AKBAR'S SYSTEM.

Speaking of the land revenue system under Akbar, Mr. Keene says: "The very successful land revenue system of British India is little more than the modification of these principles." Akbar's system has distinctive merits of its own, and even though his successors on the throne of Delhi deviated from his ideal system and innovated changes for the worse, there was a departure from even this by the early British administrators of India. When I speak of the partial survival of Akbar's land revenue system I only mean the changes introduced in the machinery of revenue administration and the setting aside of Akbar's lenient and laudable system of revenue collection by his immediate successors, while recognizing the principles underlying his system as perpetuated by the British administrators of to-day. I now proceed to state the general changes introduced by the later Mughals into the system of Akbar, while reserving the treatment of the system prevalent under them for a fuller discussion later on.

At the outset it is well to remember that by the time of Aurangzib the fifteen *Subas* of Akbar became twenty-one, since Tatta, Kashmir and Orissa, originally included by Akbar in the *Subas* of Multan, Kabul and Bengal respectively, were separated while the *Subas* of the Deccan became six instead of the original three. The framework of Akbar was to some extent retained, but several changes were effected in the designations of officers and the functions performed by them, while the spirit of Akbar's system was distorted.

A segregation was made in the functions of the *Sipah-Salar*, who was the governor of the *Suba* under Akbar. Two distinct officers sprang up, the *Subadar* who has the control of the military affairs of the province, and the *Diwan* who mainly occupied his time with revenue affairs. No direct provision was made by Akbar for a segregation like this, but slight traces of it can be seen in the different functions performed by his *Amilguzar* and *Faujdar* who jointly managed the affairs of a district.

Another change is to be seen in the functions discharged by the *Amilguzar*. The *Ain* indifferently uses *Amil* and *Amilguzar* for a single officer. In the instructions to the *Amilguzar* it says : "He shall acquaint himself with, and maturely consider the conduct of former *Amils*; and if they appear to have been guilty of inconsiderateness or dishonesty towards the husbandman, he must strive to remedy the evils they have occasioned." On Akbar's *Amilguzar* fell the main burden of revenue administration, while the *Amil* of later times was totally eclipsed by the provincial *Diwan*.

As regards the sub-divisional officers, the *Amin* and the *Karori*, some changes were introduced. Under Akbar the *Amin* was the main spring of administration. His function was to strike a compromise between the State demanding the revenue and the individual paying it, and the word literally means "an umpire, an arbitrator, a trustee for others". whereas under Aurangzib the *Amin* becomes the executive subordinate of the *Amil.* As for the *Karori* he is the actual collector of revenue under Akbar. The *Amin* assessed and the *Karori* collected. As Mr. Moreland puts it, the *Karori* under Akbar is a "colonization officer", whereas under Aurangzib he became a sub-collector.

As for the so-called "local authorities", the *Chaudhari* and the *Muqaddam*, who were headmen of the pargana and the village respectively and the *Qanungo* and *Putwari* who were registrars in the same order, Akbar put special stress upon their labours, whereas the attitude of the later Mughals towards these officials was one of suspicion and distrust.

Under the later Mughals, the spirit of Akbar's land revenue policy was totally avoided. Though innovations were introduced for the worse by the descendants of Akbar the system was to some extent preserved, but with the death of Aurangzib the system thoroughly collapsed, and it required half a century for it to reclaim its recognition under administration of early British Governors-General of India.

The general changes may be best summarized as follows. The standard of assessment was raised from one-third to one-half of the gross produce or even more. The pressure on the peasants had been increased and the farming of State revenues was resorted to. Unlike the *Zabti* system of Akbar, *Nasaq* or summary assessment became the rule under the later Mughals. The rise of the rental system and the segregation of the fiscal from the military functions of the *Sipah-Salar* are other features of importance to be noted.

Land Revenue System under the later Mughals.

We may now pass on to the system of revenue collection under the successors of Akbar. The administration of the country under Jehangir was carried on on the lines laid down by Akbar, but a general deterioration is perceivable in it owing to his personal inferiority when compared with his illustrious father. His "habitual and excessive intemperance..............added artificial ferocity to his innate violent temper." * He was a "strange compound of tenderness and cruelty, justice and caprice, refinement and brutality, good sense and childishness."† A fitful emperor, Jehangir was sometimes "barbarously cruel" in the words of Terry, and at other times showed signs of clemency. Hawkins puts the revenue of the empire under Jehangir at fifty crores of rupees. Even though the statement seems to be far from fact, we cannot refrain from believing that the revenues under Jehangir increased greatly when compared with the ten crores of Akbar. Roe's *Journal* throws light upon this point. Speaking of the viceroy of Patan he says: "He had regal authorities to take what he list." The general change from the *Zabti* to the *Nasaq* form of revenue collection is attributed to the reign of Jehangir. Mr. Moreland suggests: ‡ "The regulation system can have had no friends in the villages except among the smaller peasants; officials must have hated it because it meant hard work with strict time limit; the 'local authorities' must have resented the reduction

* Smith: *Oxford History of India*, p. 387.

† *Ibid.*

‡ *Journal of the Royal Asiatic Society*, January 1922, pp. 28-29.

of their influence; and substantial peasants must have anticipated extortion in proportion to their ability to pay. In all probability, therefore, its continuance depended upon the driving force supplied by Akbar, and I suspect that it did not last long after his death." Besides, the segregation of the powers of the *Diwan* and the *Subadar* can be traced to his reign, and the former official was placed under the direct control of the imperial *Diwan*. It is further believed that the *Diwan* was to act as a check over the autocracy of the *Subadar*, while a mutual watch was enjoined on both these officials.

Under Shah Jahan the pressure on the peasant increased. The eulogy of Rai Bhara Mal as regards the attention of Shah Jahan to "improvements of agriculture and the collection of the revenue of the State" suggests the excessive pressure of the State's demand. The imperial expenditure multiplied fourfold, and yet the treasury was full enough to supply the fabulous expenditure of money by Shah Jahan on monumental works such as the *Taj*. How far this is a sign of exceptional national progress is a point that cannot be easily assessed.

At the death of Shah Jahan fifty *Abwabs* or illegal cesses are said to have been flourishing.* The comprehensive term *Abwab* covers all the taxes of the government, such as duties on local sales of produce, fees on the sale of moveable property, licences for plying certain trades, special imposts upon the Hindu subjects, besides perquisites for the benefit of the officials and other forced loans and subscriptions.

* Sarkar : *Mughal Administration*.

Besides, a dark background was afforded by the great famine of 1630—32 to the "prodigal expenditure and unexampled splendour of the court" and the excessive demands of the State. Abdul Hamid describes the appalling condition of the country when life was offered for a cake, when dog's flesh passed off for goat's flesh, and the "flesh of a son was preferred to his love". The writer of the *Badshah-Namah* states that the emperor opened soup-kitchens, spent a lakh and a half of rupees on charity, and remitted one-eleventh of the assessment. The remission of one-eleventh of the revenue means that efforts were made to collect the rest of the revenue when the country was reduced to the direst extremity and retained no trace of productiveness.

Bernier's gloomy remarks upon the state of affairs during the period of his travels in Hindustan from 1656 to 1668 should be taken in relation to the anarchic and stormy closing years of Shah Jahan's reign and the first decade of Aurangzib's administration. But Aurangzib was preoccupied during the early years of his reign with maintaining order and making his position secure. Hence, Bernier's account may be taken broadly as representing a state of affairs at the close of Shah Jahan's reign.

In his *Letter to Colbert* Bernier gives a graphic account of the state of affairs in Hindustan. "Of the vast tracts of country constituting the empire of Hindustan, many are little more than sand, or barren mountains, badly cultivated and thinly peopled; and even a considerable portion of good land remains untilled for want of labourers; many of whom perish in consequence of the bad treatment they experience from the

governors. These poor people, when incapable of discharging the demands of their rapacious lords, are not only deprived of means of subsistence but are bereft of their children who are carried away as slaves. Thus it happens that many of the peasantry, driven to despair by so execrable a tyranny, abandon the country, and seek a more tolerable mode of existence either in towns or in camps; as bearers of burdens, carriers of water, or servants to horsemen. Sometimes they fly to the territories of a Raja, because there they find less oppression, and are allowed greater degree of comfort." *
"The country is ruined by the necessity of defraying the enormous charges required to maintain the splendour of a numerous court, and pay a large army maintained for the purpose of keeping the people in subjection. No adequate idea can be conveyed of the sufferings of that people. The cudgel and the whip compel them to incessant labour for the benefit of others; and driven to despair by every kind of cruel treatment, their revolt or their flight is only prevented by the presence of a military force."†

Again, Bernier speaks of the practice of "selling different governments for immense sums in hard cash" and the absolute authority of "timariots, governors or contractors" over the helpless, oppressed and the aggrieved peasant. The iniquities suffered by the peasants are to some extent mitigated at the capital and its neighbourhood since any serious act of outrage on the part of the officials cannot be kept from the ear of the

* *Travels in the Mogal Empire*, p. 205 (Edited by Archibald and Smith).

† *Travels*, p. 230.

emperor. "The governor is the absolute lord in the strict sense of the word" capable to "extract oil out of sand" with the sole and unrestricted authority of deciding controversies with his cane and caprice.*

But even this tyrant has some redeeming features. The sovereign as the sole fountain of justice is best exemplified in him, equitable considerations apart. Notwithstanding Shah Jahan's love of power and show and pleasure, he never relaxed the control of the administration of the country, and even introduced important changes such as the survey of the Deccan. Khafi Khan's comparative estimate of Akbar and Shah Jahan may be accepted. If Akbar is famous as conqueror and lawgiver, Shah Jahan is noted for "the order and arrangement of his territory and finance, and the good administration of every department of the State".†

We may now pass on to the system of administration of land revenue under Aurangzib. Under him it was worse, since his control over his subordinates was anything but appreciable, which was further aggravated by his habitual distrust of his officers. The main sources for our estimate of Aurangzib's revenue policy are the *Furmans* granted by him to Rashik Das and Muhammad Hashim. Both of these *Furmans* indicate that the pressure on the peasant had increased. In the *Furman* addressed to Muhammad Hashim the following passage is to be found:‡ "At the beginning of the year, inform yourself as

* *Travels*, p. 236.

† *Cf.* Elphinstone: *History*, p. 585.

‡ *Journal of the Royal Asiatic Society*, January 1922, p. 26.

far as possible about the condition of the peasant, and whether they are engaged in cultivation or abstaining from it. If they have the means to cultivate, ply them with inducements and encouragements, and show them any favour they desire. But if it be found that, in spite of having means to cultivate and of a favourable season, they are abstaining from cultivation, then you should urge and threaten them, and make use of force and the whip (*Zarab*)." Inducements and encouragements are not necessary if the people were left to cultivate their lands at ease, while using force and the whip means the cultivation of land under coercion. The above quotations from Bernier and certain clauses of the *Furmans* show the desertion and flight of cultivators from their lands, which must have been necessarily done to escape extortionate treatment. The preamble to the *Furman* addressed to Rashik Das describes the existing system as follows :—*

> "The *Amins* assess the bulk of the villages and purganas at the beginning of the year on a consideration of the produce of the *Sal-i-Kamil Wa Sal-i-Muttasil*,† the culturable areas, the conditions and the resources of the peasants and other data ;
>
> "And should the peasants of any village refuse this procedure they assess the revenue on them at harvest by the procedure of measurement (*Jarib*) or estimation (*Kankut*) ;

* *Journal of the Royal Asiatic Society*, January 1922, p. 27.

† "The past year and the present year preceding it", according to Sarkar, or "the produce of the standard year and the most recent year" according to Moreland.

> "And in some tracts (*Qariab*), where the peasants are known to be poor and to lack capital, they employ the procedure of crop division (*Ghallabakhsh*), at the rate of half, or one-third or two-fifths or more or less."

From this passage it will be evident that threats to some extent made the process of revenue collection easier. Measurement left a great scope for extortion under the mediæval methods of survey, and the villagers were in constant fear of the swarms of surveyors that might be let loose upon them.

Under Aurangzib *Nasaq* was the rule. The farming of the revenues was common since it was easier. The peasants must consent to the demands made by the State or else a resort was taken to *Paimaish* which was in itself more dreaded by them. Besides, the conditions in the *Furmans* provided for the payment of the revenue in cash. The *Furmans* provided for remissions to be granted in case of calamities that befell the country between the time of assessment and the date of collection at harvest. But the strict orders to officials to have a scrutinizing eye on the details of calamities, the utter disregard of the local Qanungos, Putwaries and other "local authorities" enjoined upon them, and the "adjusting entries" which were often made use of, suggested the existence of a certain amount of fraud.

There was a perennial struggle on the part of the administration of Aurangzib to prevent the assignees of lands from realizing extra amounts other than their stipulated incomes. But the struggle was not the outcome of the genuine desires on the part of the government to prevent perquisites from being exacted altogether; rather, their constant desire to see those collections being sent to the imperial treasury promoted the government to have a strict watch on the realizations of the timariots. The special injunctions to the provincial *Diwans* required them to see every *Dam* of revenue collected by revenue officials reach the imperial treasury by seizing the local rough accounts of villages, and comparing them with the returns despatched by their immediate revenue subordinates.

We may now compare the revenues of Aurangzib with those of his predecessors. Akbar demanded one-third of the produce realized by the cultivators while abolishing various vexatious taxes and granting remission. Aurangzib generally demanded one-half of the produce, nearly all the surplus which the peasant possessed over and above the actual cost of production. Especially in Guzerat, half and at times three-fourths was taken by the State. The preamble to the *Furman* already quoted points to the fact that revenue collection was pressed as far as it was practicable; either half or one-third, "either more or less"—it does not matter! The conditions of the people may be described in the words of Prophet Joel: "That which the palmerworm hath left hath the locust eaten; and that which the locust hath left hath the cankerworm eaten; and that which the cankerworm hath left, the caterpillar hath eaten."* Even though the farming of the revenues is not mentioned in the *Furmans* it was a circumstance which was widely prevalent in mediæval India.† The

* *The Book of Joel*, I, 4. (Old Testament. Authorized Version.)

† *Cf.* Bernier's statements quoted *infra.*

fact that the revenues of the empire greatly increased under Aurangzib when compared with the extent of the imperial dominion is best illustrated by the table of revenues for the individual reigns of the Mughal sovereigns. It represents the gross revenues of the Mughal empire at the various dates mentioned which include other sources of revenue than the land revenue and is taken from the appendices to Dr. Edward Thomas' *Revenue Resources, etc., of the Mogul Empire:*

Period	Reign	Rupees
A.D. 1594	Akbar	14,19,09,576
A.D. 1648	Shah Jahan	22,00,00,000
A.D. 1654	Aurangzib	26,74,39,702
Some year between 1656-1667	Bernier's return	22,59,35,500
Date uncertain but held to be between 1667–1691	Official returns	35,64,14,398
A.D. 1697	Aurangzib	38,62,46,802
A.D. 1707	Aurangzib	30,17,96,859

From this table it will be evident that the revenues of Aurangzib amounted at one time to nearly three times those of Akbar.

The rise of the rental system was a prominent feature about the revenue system of Aurangzib. In Akbar's administrative system there are no hints about the prevalence of the rental system, while no claim was made by the State upon land that was not cultivated. But under Aurangzib holders of land were liable to payment at a definite rate of assessment whether the land was cultivated or not. This state of affairs is traceable to the disappearance of the regulation system of Akbar and the usual prevalence of summary assessment which was convenient to officers and leading landholders, while further convenience led to the adoption of the system of cash rents.

The excessive prevalence of assignments and the farming of governments in mediæval India lead us to examine the origin and nature of the zemindar, the Jagir and the system of revenue-farming. It should be remembered that the general appearance of intermediaries was made possible by the prevalence of summary assessments, the lavish grants of assignments, and the practice of farming State revenues. The zemindar was originally an intermediary between the State and the individual peasant for the speedy collection of revenue and was allowed a commission for his labours. Later the zemindars became the immediate masters of the peasants and a clause in the *Furmans* of Aurangzib provided for *Izara* or speculative leases.

The *Jagir* system presumably originated in the distribution of the newly conquered and occupied lands by the chief of a horde among his followers and relatives. Bernier observes that * "the *King*, the proprietor of the land, makes over a certain quantity to military men as an equivalent for their pay; and this grant is called *Jah-Gir*, or as in Turkey, *Timar*; the word *Jah-Gir* signifying the spot from which to draw, or the place of salary." This is a reference to the apportioning of *Jagirs* to persons holding *Mansabs* or commissions in the army.

* *Travels*, p. 224.

Allauddin paid the army musters in cash, while under Firuj Shah the granting of *Jagirs* became the law. Akbar once again reverted to cash payments, while under his successors the granting of *Jagirs* became the general feature.

The nature of the system of farming is best described in the words of Elphinstone: * "The government of provinces in such cases is conferred on the person who engages to give security for the largest annual payment into the treasury. This contractor in like manner farms his sub-divisions to the highest bidder; and these last, in their turn, contract with the headmen for fixed payments from the villages, leaving each of them to make what profit he can for himself. By these means the natural defender of the cultivator becomes himself the principal oppressor; and, if the headman refuses the terms offered to him, the case is made worse by the transfer of his office to any stranger who is willing to accept the contract." With this passage must be taken the already cited verse from the Prophet Joel if we want to clearly understand the nature of the system. The farming of revenues was prevalent throughout mediæval India. *Ibn Batuta* travelling in A.D. 1333 speaks of the conferring of governments upon people. Speaking about the Governor of Lanari he states that "the collections of this town are sixty lakhs annually...........to the Governor pertains one-twentieth of this. On such *condition* the sovereign *confers* governments, (the grantees) taking one-twentieth of the revenues." † From this passage it is clear that the

* *History*, p. 78.

† *Journal of the Royal Asiatic Society*, July 1887, p. 398.

farming of revenues or the conferring of governments on condition prevailed as early as the beginning of the fourteenth century. Besides, the fixing of the revenue at sixty lakhs on a single town shows the abnormal collections made by the Government. We are already familiar with the remarks of Bernier and they need not be repeated once again. Suffice it to say that the farming of the revenues reached its highest pitch by the middle of the seventeenth century. Even as late as the close of the eighteenth century we see the system of farming revenues by Warren Hastings. By putting certain tracts of land to auction he realized the revenue from middlemen to whom the revenues were farmed, and this was intended as a makeshift for his hurried quinquennial 'settlement' of 1772-77. The evil effects of this system have already been described. *More was paid* than the stipulated sums and hence the misery of the people was aggravated.

Murshid Quli Khan's Settlement of the Deccan.

A word or two may be needed to explain a separate treatment given to the settlement of the Deccan by Murshid Quli Khan. In the first place, the system was totally confined to the Deccan. Being an outlying province the system of revenue collection prevailing there is not quite consonant with the one existing in the plains of Hindustan. Secondly, the system affords a bold contrast to the methods of revenue collection by Shah Jahan and remains an administrative enigma, so far as the nature of revenue collection under Aurangzib is viewed in relation to his subadarship of the Deccan and his position as the Emperor of Delhi. Besides, we find a relief in Murshid Quli Khan after seeing the unpleasant nature of things existing in Shah Jahan's time and after. Murshid Quli Khan was a brilliant student of the revenue system of Raja Todar Mal, and imbibed its true spirit. Even though he "*plagiarised*" from the system of Todar Mal—if ever there is plagiarising in the field of administration, his system remains laudable against the travesties of the ideal form of revenue system handed on to posterity by Akbar, Jehangir and Shah Jahan on the one hand, and by Aurangzib on the other.

Aurangzib's viceroyalty of the Deccan marks an epoch in the history of the revenue administration in Southern India. It stands as a contrast to the existing systems of revenue collection all over India, and offers a bold model for copying by later sovereigns in the Deccan. When Aurangzib first became Viceroy of the Deccan he saw a wretched state of conditions prevailing. Lands were not efficiently cultivated, revenues of the State were scanty, the extortion on the part of the Government great, and the peasant's lot miserable. All this was further aggravated by the penury of the people.

The wretched state of affairs is attributable to the governors appointed to manage the affairs of the country. A frequent succession of short viceroyalties aggravated the appalling situation of the country. It is stated that in eight years there were six viceroys.* Even Aurangzib was frequently displaced in his viceroyalty by his fitful father. But he had under his régime an industrious and benevolent revenue administrator, Murshid Quli Khan,

* Sarkar: *Aurangzib*, Vol. I, p. 178.

who combined in his person "the valour of a soldier with the administrative capacity of a civil servant."*

When Murshid Quli Khan was appointed Diwan of Balaghat or High Lands—an administrative division of the Deccan effected by Aurangzib, he found the state of the peasants wretched. Several abuses had crept in during the first and second viceroyalties of Aurangzib between A.D. 1644—1653, and especially the abominable tyrant Khan-i-Dauran's death was "hailed as a divine deliverance".† Utter chaos prevailed in the Deccan and the absence of system in matters of revenue collection left the people at the mercy of rapacious and greedy revenue underlings. And there was a general desertion of lands by the people.

Murshid Quli Khan set himself to ameliorate the condition of the people and extended to Balaghat the system of Todar Mal—a panacea for revenue maladies. The system as changed by local conditions was afterwards borrowed by the rest of the Deccan. He gathered all the scattered ryots by deputing wise *Amins* and honest surveyors to make a minute and impartial survey of the land, appointed *Muqaddams* of character to villages who had lost their headmen, granted *Taqavvi* loans in case of peasants who were incapable of buying the necessary 'plant' for agriculture, and maintained the efficiency and equity of the system by strict personal supervision. "The honest and God-fearing *Diwan* often dragged the measuring chain himself with his own hands" to prevent corruption and partiality. Above all he gave due

* *Ibid.*, p. 190.

† Smith: *Oxford History*, p. 418.

consideration to local conditions. He fixed a lump payment in certain cases, resorted to metayarship in other cases, at the rate of half the produce in case of crops depending upon rainfall and one-third in case of crops depending upon wells or canals. Even here the standard of Government's share was fixed at one-fourth, and a *Jarib* or survey was made for the fixation of assessment rates according to the area cultivated and the nature of crop grown. Here, as regards the scale of assessment by Murshid Quli Khan, it may be curious for us to note what logicians call a chance coincidence of phenomena between it and the injunctions of Sukra about the share of revenue that is to be demanded by the State with regard to lands depending upon varying sources of nutrition. Sukra says "The king should realize one-third, one-fourth or one-half from places which are irrigated by tanks, canals and wells, by rains and rivers respectively."*

On the whole Murshid Quli Khan's settlement was a grand success. Personal superintendence and constant vigilance made the system efficient and excellent. There was a rapid improvement in agriculture, a proportionate increase of revenue, a consequent abundance of grain and a cheapness of the common articles of consumption.†

* IV. ii. 227. Prof. Benoy Kumar Sarkar's version. But the Telugu version by Puranapanda Mallia Sastri is more correct. *Vide* his translation, pp. 132 33.

† See Prof. Sarkar's *Aurangzib*, Vol. I, pp. 189 195.

CHAPTER IV.

State's Proprietorship of the Soil.

To people accustomed to the notion of absolute right possessed by an individual in his private property under the British Government, the State's proprietorship of land looks strange. It did look strange, indeed, to Bernier whose observations about it in the days of the later Mughals leads us to a discussion of State proprietorship of land.

The undisputed right of the Government as the sole proprietor of the soil was recognized throughout India prior to the advent of the British Government. But there are a few exceptions. In ancient India there is no perfect right of property vested in a single body in cases where there are village communities and permanent tenants,* and ancient Indian law recognizes no freeholders except in Malabar and certain other regions in the peninsula. Munro found documentary evidence as to the existence of private property in land in North Kanara going back for a thousand years, and in Carnatic Tanjore and Madura.† "In Canara, Malabar and Travancore, the land is held in absolute property by single individuals, subject to a fixed payment to the State." ‡

We may now pause for a moment for the further evidence that can be gathered from ancient Hindu

* Elphinstone : *History*, p. 79.

† Gleig : *Life*, as quoted by Vincent Smith, *Oxford History*, Foot-note, pp. 562-3.

‡ Elphinstone : *History*, p. 76.

sources which can easily refute the suggestion derived from a perusal of Elphinstone—that there is no perfect right of property vested in single bodies and that ancient Indian law recognizes no freeholders.

Sage Sukra observes as regards the origin of kingship: "(At first) when the world was without a king, and in consequence the people fled in all directions on account of diverse dangers that befell them, the Almighty (Brahma) created *for the protection of these*, a king with everlasting particles drawn from Indra, Anila, Yama, Arka, Agni, Varuna, Chendra and Kubera.

"Just as Indra, by his penance, is the lord of the animate and inanimate, and receiving sacrifices, protects well the world, a king, by virtue of his penance, becomes the lord of all and receiving tributes from his subjects carefully protects them."

"The king is made by Brahma to be the servant of his subjects by reason of his receiving payments in the shape of tribute; and he is made lord in consideration of his duty to protect them." †

From these passages it is evident that kingship was of divine origin. The king, being created in an opportune time when anarchy was rampant and lawlessness was rife, was vested naturally with unlimited power over the lives and property of individuals composing the population of his dominion. Hence we may apply to such a system of government the term—Theocracy—excluding from the scope of the term the presence of a compact, co-ordinate and co-existent

* *Sukranitisara*, Ch. I, ver. 71-73 † *Ibid.*, I, ver. 188.

priestly class, like that of the mediæval church in Europe, since even though the Brahmins formed the chief power behind the throne, they never formed an *imperium in imperio*. Here we are now obsessed with one of the prominent historical paradoxes: How is it that the king became the sole proprietor of the soil with the summary disposal of his subjects' rights and lives since he was only Lord paramount, the 'Imperator Terrene', in a moment of chaotic circumstances? The probable answer may be that he collected round him certain loyal subjects and distributed among them the whole land and left it with them as a sort of perpetual usufruct. As civil government progressed and as people recognized the advantages of becoming peaceful and settled, they came to realize their vested interests and clung to them tenaciously—all the while paying some tribute to the regal fisc for the maintenance of the government and the king himself. Hence Sukra's seemingly incompatible appellations of the king being at once the servant and lord of men.

In the *Brihaspati Dharmasastra*, popularly attributed to the sixth or seventh century A.D., the following verse is found: "Should any such partner in trade happen to die through want of proper care, his goods must be shown (and delivered) to officers appointed by the king." * The reference is to the corporate and joint stock undertakings in ancient India. May it not suggest that right of the king over the private property after the person's demise?

* *Brih*. XIV. 11, quoted in Majumdar's *Corporate Life in Ancient India*, p. 31.

But by the time of the seventh century private property seems to have been clearly taken cognizance of. In the *Sukranitisara* is a passage which draws a distinction between *Sahaja* and *Adhika* incomes.* "A *Sahaja* income is that which comes permanently to a person every day, month or year and which accrues to a person permanently every day, month or year either from his ancestral property or from his own work.

"*That which is got from the ancestral property is called the best Sahaja income.* *Adhika* or additional income includes profit, interest, fees for officiating in sacrifices, rewards, salary and other income got in a similar way." By this passage we can evidently illustrate the forthcoming definition of property since the mention and the distinction between *Sahaja* and *Adhika* income is an ample testimony to the point in question.

Mr. K. V. Rangaswami Aiyangar has clearly pointed out after careful investigation that "the ancient Indian State very decidedly recognized the institution of *private* property and *individual* proprietary right over all forms of wealth, including land."† Again, it points out in a note relating to the conception of an *ideal* prince by Kautilya and Machiavelli that according to their theories the king "should not unduly interfere with the property rights of his subjects, for '*A man will sooner forgive the slaying of his father than the confiscation of his patrimony!*'"‡ From these passages it is evident that private property is one of the foremost objects of a

* II. 329 and 330-1.

† Sir Subramanya Ayyar's Lecture 1914: *Consideration on Some Aspects of Ancient Indian Polity*, p. 72.

‡ *Ibid.*, Appendix, p. 149.

man's longing and was fully acceded to by ancient Hindu kings, while they were recognized by principles of equity.

Coming to our *Ain* we find the perfect right of the ancient Hindus in private property. Even though Abul Fazl speaks of the escheatability of property in case of default in payment of State revenue * as was prevalent in the customs of the Hindus, he goes on with a detailed enumeration of the ways in which moieties of the property left behind by a deceased person should be enjoyed by those near and dear to him according to individual claims, ultimately leaving the king to enjoy it in case of the failure of proper persons to share it. From all these data gathered from different sources relating to different times it is evident that there are clear traces of the existence of private property and individual proprietorship in ancient India, even though they were at times eclipsed by the demands of the greedy kings.

"Who but a tyrant (a name expressive of everything which can vitiate and degrade human nature) could think of seizing on the property of men, unaccused, unheard and untried, by wholesale proscriptions by hundreds and thousands together? Who that had not lost every trace of humanity could think of casting down men of exalted rank and sacred function, some of them of an age to call at once for reverence and compassion—of casting them from the highest situation in the commonwealth wherein they are maintained by their own landed property, to a state of indigence, depression and contempt."

* *Ain.*, p. 745.

This passage* warns us against the injustice that can be caused by the caprice of an emperor who is not always infallible with the prerogative of Summary Disposal.

" Property in land seems to consist in the exclusive use and absolute disposal of the soil in perpetuity; together with the right to alter or destroy the soil itself where such an operation is possible."† But no such rights were recognized in the time of the Mughals, and even in the Hindu kingdom of Vizianagar the *Raya*, besides reserving to himself some crown lands such as the *Khalsa* of the Moguls, had the sole proprietorship of the soil and could deprive at will even eminent nobles of their assignments. Bernier points out that the sole right of the property as vested in the hands of the government makes the ryots lose their respect for private property " which is the basis of all that is good and useful in the world " and consequently proves injurious to the State itself. And Edmund Burke speaks with reference to the summary confiscation of Church property in France.

Exclaiming that "if this exclusive and baneful right prevailed, far different would be the real riches of the sovereigns of *Europe*, and the loyalty and fidelity with which they are served. They would soon reign over solitude and deserts, over mendicants and barbarians."‡ Bernier proceeds to a discussion of the rights of private property. Stating "that the absence of it among the

* Burke : *Reflections on the French Revolution*. Edited by Selby, pp. 117–18.

† Elphinstone : *History*, p. 79.

‡ *Travels*, p. 232.

people is injurious to the best interest of the sovereign himself," and giving a graphic description of the appalling condition of the people under the grinding control of the timariots, Bernier proceeds: "The peasant cannot avoid asking himself this question: 'Why should I toil for a tyrant who may come to-morrow and lay his rapacious hand upon all I possess and value, without leaving me, if such should be his humour, the means to drag on my miserable existence,'—The Timariots, Governors and Revenue contractors, on their part reason in this manner: 'Why should the neglected state of this land create unrest in our minds? and why should we expend our own money and time to render it fruitful? We may be deprived of it in a single moment, and our exertions would benefit neither ourselves nor our children. Let us draw from the soil all the money we can, though the peasant should starve and abscond, and we should leave it, when commanded to quit, a dreary wilderness" * and concludes his *Letter to Colbert* in the following manner: "Yes, my lord, to conclude briefly, I must repeat it; take away the right of private property in land, and you introduce, as a sure and necessary consequence, tyranny, slavery, injustice, beggary and barbarism; the ground will cease to be cultivated and become a dreary wilderness; in a word, the road will be opened to the ruin of kings and the destruction of nations. It is the hope by which a man is animated, that he shall retain the fruits of his industry, and transmit them to his descendants, that forms the main foundation of everything excellent and beneficial in

* *Travels*, p. 227.

this sublunary state; and if we take a review of the different kingdoms of the world, we shall find that they prosper or decline according as this principle is acknowledged or condemned; in a word, it is the prevalence of neglect of this principle which changes and diversifies the face of the earth."* Besides the appeal which they make to our sentments, these passages have the indirect testimonies of various records of the age, and are corroborated by clauses in the *Furmans* granted by Aurangzib to resort to inducements and other encouragements where the peasants show overtures of discontent and resolve to fly away from their tenements. And we are already familiar with the ephemeral character of the Muslim society of the times when the fortunes amassed by the exertions of a single enterprising individual reverted to the State soon after his death, while the escheatability of land in case of default in the payment of revenue is a recognized fact.

The great importance attached by Bernier to the individual's right of property is just, and more is the description true as regards the conditions prevailing in the Mughal empire. But to-day the British administrators have actually recognized the elementary rights of individuals to enjoy the fruits of their labours and perpetuate their interests, so that the Bengal Tenancy Act of 1885, the Act of 1887 and other such Acts were passed making direct statutory legislations protecting the tenants from eviction and enhancement of rent, while giving them compensation for improvements and recognizing the principles of fixity of tenure and judicial rents.

* P. 238.

CHAPTER V.

Currency System of the Mughal Empire.

A survey of the land revenue system of the Mughal Empire will be better understood if a bird's-eye view of the currency system of the times is presented. Even though to speak of the currency *system* of the Mughal Empire amounts to a misnomer, the student of the Mughal history derives much desirable information from a study of the general nature of the coins issued by the Mughal sovereigns. A study of the merits or otherwise of the coins of the times is essential inasmuch as it affords us an idea whether the peasants and ignorant folk of the age were not labouring under disadvantageous circumstances as regards the issue and circulation of the legal tender, whether the country was not inflated with an excessive issue of the circulating medium, whether there is any scope for the operation of what is generally known as Gresham's Law. Further, a study of the nature of the currency in the Mughal Empire is of perennial interest to financiers and students of economics, since it best illustrates the principle of the "progressive deterioration of monetary denominations"; especially in India.

But the ground to tread is not smooth and trustworthy, and many points of importance are at times conjectural and hazardous. The material is in itself scanty at times, and often complicated, and hence hard to draw upon. Only sundry and scattered passages in the records of foreign travellers, and indigenous compilers of *tarikhs* throw some gleam of light upon the imperfect presentation by the *Ain-i-Akbari* of the currency system of Akbar which served as the model to a great extent for subsequent issues of coinage by the later Mughals.

No student of Mughal history can adequately thank Prof. Shahpurshah Hormasji Hodivala for the indefatigable energy he expended in producing a monumental work, his *Historical Studies in Mughal Numismatics*, forming the second part of the *Occasional Memoirs of the Numismatic Society of India.* Prof. Hodivala, with all his powers of exegesis and decipherment, has ransacked all the available material, indigenous as well as foreign, in the production of colossal work, and reminds one of the labours of Prof. Jadunath Sarkar, the real Gibbon of the Decline and Fall of the Mughal Empire. Much of the material manipulated in the following observations is derived from his work, while my homage to the *Ain-i-Akbari* is patent on the surface.

The minting of coins during the flourish of the Mughal Empire is not confined to the capital city alone. In the days of Akbar, there are throughout the empire four mints for the coinage of gold, silver and copper; nine mints for the mintage of silver and copper; and twenty-eight mints for the coinage of copper only.* Even though there might have been changes in the location and number of mints in the reigns of the later Mughals, the prevalence of provincial mints is a fact beyond dispute. A curious point to note about these mints is that coins and medals were struck even at mints far removed from the capital, when the emperor was on

Ain., p. 25.

a tour or visit to the town where the mint was situated for the purposes of *Nisar*, or scattering of coins and tokens among the curious rabble of ignorant town and village folk as a tangible attestation, real or assumed, of his love for his subjects in order to win their loyalty and buy their hearts.

Here we may stop for a moment and try to get at the nature of mintages for the purposes of *Nisar*. Etymologically the word *Nisar* signifies the act of scattering, the thing scattered, a small coin distributed at weddings.* It is one of the most common words to be met with in the Mughal chronicles, reminding us of one of the Pan-Asiatic customs of antiquity where a profuse distribution of largesse was made either in the form of coins or of precious stones waved round the head of the emperor or some other principal dignitary of state, and thrown among the crowds that scramble for them on important occasions such as a royal progress through the country, a munificent wedding, a birthday anniversary and the like, and the weighing of the emperor's own person (known in Sanskrit as *Tulabhar*) against precious stones and coins which were then distributed among his subjects. Not only coins but also imitation fruits—Sir Thomas Roe saw the distribution of "two chargers of *hollow almonds* of *gold* and silver mingled", and flowers were distributed on such occasions. The ostensible dignity of the regal prerogative which often produced an unscrupulous lavishness, the perpetual hankering after the realization of the commutation of the subjects' fidelity for his largesse, and a constant desire to appease Nemesis

* Hodivala : *Historical Studies*, etc. p. 176.

when a sudden and vast store of riches was realized by him as seen in the case of the weighment of his own person make a king resort to the distribution of *Nisar.* Later, by the time of Jehangir an actual coin, the *Nisar,* was struck mainly for such purposes.

Unlike the present-day Government of India the Mughal sovereigns never reserved to themselves the mintage of coins on their account. It was then a free or gratuitous coinage. An inducement was given to the people to bring bullion to the mints and take away coins instead by the profit which they can realize by so doing. The *Ain-i-Akbari* gives elaborate accounts indicating the profit which a person can derive by taking bullion to the mint.*

Just as the standard gold is said in modern days to be eleven-twelfths fine, the fineness of coins in the time of Akbar is spoken of in terms of *Bannies,* ten *Unnies* fine being the standard gold. A peculiar point to note here is the fact that the quantity of bullion taken for purposes of minting a particular coin varies according to its fineness. Even at the present day, with highly organized mints and superior dyes, a so-called weight-remedy of two-tenths of a grain is allowed for every sovereign weighing 123.27447 grains. But in the days of Akbar with his hopelessly crude mints and unscientific management—yet they afforded the ideal for the age, a weight-remedy of one *Mashah* was taken for every round gold *Muhr* weighing eleven *Mashahs.*

Another disadvantage is that the coins of the day were hammered and not milled. Just as the Bank of

* Pp. 30-33.

England now discounts 1½*d*. for every ounce of gold brought down to it for the purpose of taking down coins instead, to cover the charges of its labour, and to make a profit out of the transaction, the seigniorage under Akbar amounted to six per cent in the case of gold,* while a like amount was taken for the actual cost of minting known in modern days as *Brassage*, as M. Chavalior was pleased to name it so.

We may now turn to the fineness in the coins of the Mughal sovereigns. Mughal coinage is remarkably known for the markedly smaller proportion of alloy in them than that of the present-day system of coinage. And absolute purity of the coinage in the Mughal Empire has been the occasion for foreign travellers to shower panegyrics upon them. The modern methods of assaying and quantitative analysis are able to substantiate the seemingly undeserving and enthusiastic exclamations of foreign travellers. In one instance of the forty-four coins assayed, no less than fourteen were found to be absolutely pure without a single grain of alloy even at the present day, all of them tracing their origin back to different reigns and different mints. And this is indeed a remarkable fact. The cumulative testimony of foreign travellers is to the point. Edmund Terry says: "The coin there is more pure than in any part of the world, being *(as they report)* of pure silver without any alloy." Herbert says that "the Mahmudi and the rupees were of good silver"; Mundy, "the current coin is of good gold, silver, copper"; Thavenot, "the silver money of the Great Mogul is finer than any other"; Fryer, "the most refined and purest

* *Ain.*, p. 30.

form alloy in the world"; and Ovington remarks that "the gold of Surat is so very fine that twelve and fourteen per cent may be often gained by bringing it to Europe".*

An important feature to note is that the Mughal rulers often maintained a very high sort of uniformity of coinage throughout the vast empire. Not only coins issued from the various provincial mints, but also those minted under successive sovereigns with varying regulations offer us a consensus of uniformity, and James Princep sums up the evidence, after tabulating the disadvantage specimens of coins belonging to the later Mughals "that Mughal Emperors maintained a great sort of uniformity in the currency of their vast empire".

The careful student of Mughal numismatics cannot fail to perceive the gradual deterioration of mintages during the period of Mughal decline. The reasons for such a phenomenon are not far to seek. The imperfection of the technical processes of the day as regards the minting of coins, the vast room for fabrication left for unscrupulous and greedy goldsmiths inasmuch as the coins of the day were only hammered, the gross dishonesty of the mint masters and treasurers in tampering with integrity of the coinage, the "mean mercenary wretches" as the *Ain-i-Akbari* calls them,† the general practice of sweating and clipping which eventually brings about the operation of Gresham's Law, the deliberate lowering of the standard of fineness and weight by dishonest *Daroghas* in whose hands was placed the management of the mints, the lack of the necessary incentive to efficient administration by the ruler himself which leads to the

* Hodivala: *Historical Studies, etc.*, pp. 240—41.

† P. 27.

degeneracy of oriental despotisms, and above all, the pernicious practice of farming the revenues of the mint first to be seen in the reign of Farrukhsiyar (A.D. 1713-1719)—all these conditions engendered the progressive deterioration of mintages under the later Mughals.

India as it is at present was bimetallic even in the reigns of the Mughal sovereigns, even though we do not subscribe to the theory of the prevalence of a bimetallic or composite standard in those days. No mention of a single kind of coin which is not unlimited legal tender is to be found in contemporary records. All coins were unlimited legal tender as we shall see presently in the injunctions of Akbar. The absence of *system* in the general currencies of the times occasions frequent fluctuations in the ratio between the values of gold and silver. As we have already seen, Mughal coinage is gratuitous and not limited to Government account. Hence the Government has not the necessary opportunity for scrupulously maintaining a standard in the ratio between the two metals by temporarily suspending the issue, or causing the inflation of this or that kind of coinage, as occasion demands it according as they appreciate or depreciate in value. And one more point to note here is that Mughal conquerors, unlike their happy successors in power, the British people, never dissociated themselves with the causes of India, since though originally birds of passage they got themselves permanently settled in India, acquired permanent vested interests there and maintained no appreciable interests in the west to look back to or support. They have no occasion to shuffle the exchange ratios to settle profitably the accounts

6

as regards the Home charges. Hence the fluctuations in the ratio used to drift generally from one point to another.

In the days of Akbar when the *Ain-i-Akbari* was compiled the ratio of the value of gold to that of silver stood at 9.4 : 1; under Jehangir it was 12 : 1; during the reign of Shah Jehan it rose to 14 : 1¾ and the highest watermark in the depreciation of the value of silver was reached in the reign of Aurangzib when the ratio approximated 16 : 1.* This state of affairs was directly amenable to the increased output of silver during the sixteenth and the seventeenth centuries (1545-1680) which seriously affected the prosperity of India through the medium of the Portuguese and other merchants, and which ultimately saw the adoption of a silver currency for the empire in the reign of Aurangzib.†

Gresham's Law is sure to operate here. Hence the gold coinage gradually disappeared from general circulation and was only to be seen in the house of principal dignitaries of the state who can afford to manage huge transactions, while the ordinary peasant and artisan thought it lucrative either to melt the gold coin into bullion and then dispose of it against silver money or hoard it up. And this has been the actual observation of more than one traveller hailing from foreign countries to India.

We have already seen that the general currency of gold and silver coins side by side in the empire is apt to lead historians to conclude the prevalence of a bimetallic

* Hodivala: *Historical Studies, etc.*, pp. 248-251.

† *J.R.A.S.*, July 1887, p. 497.

standard in the days of the Mughal sovereigns. Such a view is erroneous. The Government authorities of those times were neither statisticians, expert economists, nor financial innovators to subscribe to this or that theory of bimetallic or monometallic standard. The very notions were quite alien and unknown to them, and the artificial limitation of the circulation of a particular coin as occasion demands it, and the fixation of a stable ratio between the two precious metals to render commerce to be carried on a sure basis were beyond their comprehension. Their ideas of economics and social history are quite astonishing to us of the twentieth century, while our theories of economics and national finance were quite inane to them, much less comprehensible. Hence to speak of the prevalence of a bimetallic *standard* in those days is nothing short of reading certain of the present-day ideas into the nature of the general circulation of gold coins in juxtaposition with the silver ones. Yet the facts stand bare before us and supply us with much covetable material.

The exchange value of the rupee under the Mughals has been stated by Sir Thomas Roe as *2s. 2d.*; while the French writers of the later times mention that one and a half *livers* are the equivalent of one rupee.* The French *liver* is now obsolete, the modern equivalent of which is the Franc, which is a little more than nine and half pence in English money. The reason for the steady fall in the value of the rupee is at hand. The great influx of silver into India by the time of Aurangzib, as we have already seen, led to a great depreciation in the

* Mr. Keene's paper, *J.R.A.S.*, July 1887.

value of silver during the days when the fabric of the Mughal Empire showed overtures of a sure decline.

To the student of Mughal numismatics a real insight into the exact value of the Mughal Tola will be of immense importance, since then alone will it be possible for him to really comprehend the import of the several statements to be met with in the contemporary records relating to the coins of the day. The *Tola* is the unit of the British ponderary system and weighs 180 grains Troy. But the *Tola* of the Mughals is generally heavier than the British Indian tola. The statements of the contemporary writers as regards its actual weight come within the compass of 155 to 190.5 grains. But these are the two extremes, the one making us think it incredible, while the other asks us to doubt it exceedingly. There never can have been a regular standard in the weight of the Mughal *Tola* as against the constant form we perceive for the English pound and the French metre. The Mughal *Tola* is based on *Ratis* and the *Ratis* are in their turn dependent upon the rice grains. To obtain a steady and scientific standard between two rice grains belonging to two different places and times is almost an impossibility, while the caprice of the Government was directly responsible for decrees that often meddled with the integrity of the coinage; Mr. Hodivala observes justly. "Whatever the merits of the old Indian system of weights and measures, and however well adopted it might have been to its environment, or the manner of thinking of the people, it was crude and empirical. The foundations of the tables were on units which had never been standardized and which were, perhaps, in their nature incapable of being reduced to uniformity."* After all this, we can safely conclude on the authority of the corroborated testimony of the contemporary writers that the weight of the Mughal *Tola* ranged somewhere between 185 and 186 grains Troy.

Having sketched out the general features of the Mughal currency we may now profitably turn to the prominent features of the numismatics during the individual reigns of Mughal sovereigns separately. Here, when I classify a certain coin as pertaining to this or that particular reign, I should not be understood as drawing a clear line of demarcation as for its vogue of circulation. On the other hand it should be understood that coin came into prominence in that particular reign, was first struck during that time, or has much to do with that particular prince; while they might have been circulating previously to that reign or after.

The reign of Babar, the genesis of the Mughal dynasty on the throne of Delhi, is the starting point of our investigation. A conqueror with a vast field for exploitation before him and a greedy rabble of fiery soldiers to satisfy behind him, Babar never had the resources necessary that could be easily realized from a settled and orderly government, nor the opportunities for making any innovations in the existing order of currency. Hence he never appears to have struck any gold money in his own name. "He was perhaps too poor to afford the luxury." Besides, during his reign we find clear traces of the general currency of foreign

* *Loc. Cit.*, p. 233.

monetary denominations as can be inferred from several passages to the like effect in the contemporary authorities and records. The *Ashrafi*, the *Shahrukhi*, the ½ *Tuman* are the three types of coins which *figure prominently in his reign.*

The *Ashrafi*, of Mameluk origin, became famous in the fifteenth century when it was finally adopted into the Egyptian currency. The original etymological meaning of it is 'noble', corresponding to the English *noble* and in course of time it came to be loosely applied to all sorts of gold coins of varying weights and values. Its value was differently given by different authorities as being 11*s.* 6*d.* and 7*s.* respectively. The *Ashrafi* is several times mentioned in the *Memoirs of Babar* and other contemporary records attesting to the plenitude of its circulation and vogue. Hence it is evident that the coins belonging to the denomination under review did away with the lack of gold coins in the reign of Babar.

The *Shahrukhi* is another coin to be frequently met with in contemporary records, and many of the accounts of State revenue during the reigns of Babar and Humayun were computed in that denomination. From these data it is evident that "it was an important, if not the most important, unit of value" during their reigns. As for its value, 2½ *Shahrukhis* went to make Akbar's rupee and it weighed about 72 grains troy of silver.

The very fact that the *Tuman* forms one of the denominations of Persian money should not lead us to conclude that the numismatics of the Mughal dynasty have nothing to do with it. Originally belonging to Iraq or Khurassan, the *Tuman* presumably came into India in the reign of Babar, and it certainly elucidates the vexed and difficult proposition of the value of the Akbari *Tankha*, while it fully illustrates the principle of the progressive deterioration in value of monetary denominations. The primary significance of the Mongolian word *Tuman* is 'myriad' or 'ten thousand', and hence it gradually came to denote a sum of money worth ten thousand *Dinars*. According to the *Akbarnama* the *Tuman* was not fixed, but was subject to local variations and has certainly gone down in value. By the time of Jehangir it was only reckoned to be worth thirty rupees, and by the time of Khafi Khan in the early part of the eighteenth century its value ran down to rupees twenty-four. "The *Tuman* was a mere money of account, and imaginary denomination with a fixed theoretical value of book-rate, but no substantial or metallic basis, and there is nothing to show that it was subject to temporary variations according to the balance of trade or the supply and demand of the precious metals."*

The reign of Humayun forms a sort of *interregnum* in the monetary history of the Mughal Empire when everything was in a sort of chaotic condition. The royal fugitive was to seek the wavering support of small potentates, while his not unbecoming rival was installed on the throne of Delhi. But even at a moment of extreme disquietude Sher Shah was able to lend a certain amount of his attention to fiscal matters. As it has been already pointed out, he reformed the currency by the issue of an abundant quantity of genuine silver money noted for its

* Hodivala : *Historical Studies, etc.*, p. 197.

integrity; while Abul Fazl grimly admits the fact that the earliest and indelible traces of ingenuity as are to be seen in the rupee of Akbar (his deliberate hero), are to be seen in the rupee financial legislation of Sher Shah.*

The reign of Akbar saw many important innovations and improvements in the monetary history of the Mughal Empire. And if ever we are justified in speaking of the currency *system* of the Mughal Empire we should support our arguments upon the injunctions and regulations of Akbar concerning the general process of minting, the administration of the mints and the standard of integrity aimed at in the mintages.

The system of coinage under Akbar is a thorough process of experimenting and evolution. Experiments were being carried on by Amir Fattullah and Raja Todar Mal about the fixation of the depreciation allowance rendered necessary by the constant wear and tear, until 1591, when Akbar decreed that the gold *Muhar* deficient by three grains and the rupee falling short by six grains should not be deemed 'right' coins and hence be accepted as bullion. This decree did away with the old evil practice of accepting degenerate coins by receiving additional bullion to make up the deficiency which left a great scope to the mint-masters—"the mean mercenary wretches" as the *Ain-i-Akbari* calls them†—to mint coins of questionable integrity and pass them off for 'right' coins before the secular eyes of ignorant village folk, thus making a sinecure of their mints at the expense

* *Ain.*, p. 23.
† P. 27.

of those innocent customers. Besides, clipping the coins was to some extent prevented.

Akbar's injunctions leave no scope for favouring a particular coin and the treasuries were to accept any coins which the people brought in to pay their dues. To read modern notions into those ancient prevalences, the coins of the day were unlimited legal tender. "No serf shall be taken upon the coins of the present reign that are of full weight" and "the coins of former reigns shall be received as bullion".* Abul Fazl, summing up the regulations of Akbar about the mintages, says: "As through the attention of the Majesty, gold and silver were brought to the greatest degree of purity; in a like manner the form of the coin was improved."†

Of the 'importal coins' mentioned in Abul Fazl's inventory of Akbar's coins there are twenty-four gold coins of which the *Lal-i-Jalali Muhr* worth ten rupees, and the round *Muhar* worth nine rupees were generally current in the empire; nine principal silver coins, besides many other minor ones, of which the *rupee* containing about 178 grains of a very high standard of silver and worth forty *dams* of copper, became the general medium of exchange and four kinds of copper coins of which the *dam* gained currency in the adjustment of accounts involving fractions of a rupee. The *dam* was further divided into twenty-five parts called *Chetels* purely for purposes of adjusting minute accounts. Besides these there are two old specimens of coins called the *Diwan*

* *Ain.*, p. 268.

† *Ibid.*, p. 17.

to be met with in the ordinary course of life in Akbar's time

"Akbar's passion for innovation has been the subject of universal remark and his fondness for neologisms often transgressed the bounds of reason and common sense. Badauni informs us that the emperor got a Brahmin named Purukhottam 'to invent particular Sanskrit names for all things in existence'."* This sort of a perpetual hankering after innovation made him meticulously struggle for contriving silly and meaningless devices for the satisfaction of his own fancy. The high sort of oriental magnificence characteristic of all sovereigns flourishing in all time and climes in the east, mingled with the usual pitch of Muhammadan ostentation, and heightened by the native powers of æsthetic appreciation, made Akbar to see everything around him in perfect array and grandiloquence. Hence his zeal for show, his passion for innovation, his catering to the promptings of his fancy.

The great noteworthy feature about Akbar's system of coinage is the so-called 'Gigantic coins' or phenomenal pieces. Foreign travellers like Hawkins and de Laet were struck with the transcendental brilliance (so it seemed to them) of these phenomenal pieces and left their testimonials full of adulatory encomiums.

Heavy stamped ingots "bearing the stamp of the assayer and the banker in evidence of their purity" have been in extensive circulation at one time in China and Central Asia. Akbar, with all his keen susceptibility for

* Hodivala: *Historical Studies, etc.*, p. 143.

innovation, struck special coins of unusual weights—of course not for general circulation. Father and son vied each with the other in the mintage of those phenomenal coins, and Jehangir mentions the presentation of gold *Muhr* weighing 1,000 tolas to Yādgar Ali, the ambassador of the ruler of Iran, while gigantic coins, though not so monstrous as the one just mentioned, are to be met with in the mintages of Shah Jahan and Aurangzib.

Akbar in his great zeal for innovation invented fanciful names for the biggest coins among the monetary denominations taken mostly from Sanskrit and the other Indian vernaculars, and actually employed a Brahmin in his service for the purpose of inventing Sanskrit names for all things in the world as we have already seen. Thus the coin *S'hansah* can be traced to the Sanskrit *Sahasra* signifying one thousand. The rationale underlying it is that this coin contained one hundred *Lal-i-Jalali Muhrs* each of which is valued at ten rupees. Thus the thousand rupees, the value of the *S'hansah*, gave it that particular name.

The mintages of these phenomenal pieces and portentous medals have occasioned a serious disagreement among the eminent numismatists as to their origin and value. Dr. Edward Thomas has postulated that they served the purpose of our present-day bank notes, especially representing higher amounts—actual coin-substitutes for our modern convertible paper money representing high values. On the other hand, General Cunningham has forwarded his theory that they were '*Nazarana Medals*', struck mainly in the interests of the big nobles in the empire, who can pay a single stamped ingot or a portentous medal more conveniently than a thousand *Muhrs* in lieu of their dues to the crown. Both these theories are no longer tenable. The one is not a palpable fact, while the other is only conjectural and hazardous, but both bear the authority of eminent men well versed to pronounce a judgment.

The possible origin and nature of those medals we are now to infer. A grandiloquent affectation at magnificence in glorying about the mintage of gigantic coins, and an arduous desire to exalt the empire in the eyes of foreign ambassadors by presenting them with such phenomenal pieces made the Mughal sovereign decree the minting of such portentous coins. Besides those gigantic coins served as stores of value. The revenue resources of the Mughal Empire often being in excess of the actual expenditure; the habitual practice of hoarding up valuable metals inasmuch as the profitable systems of modern banking and co-operative concerns were unknown to them; the constant demand for a cash reserve which can rise equal to the occasion in any moment of financial crisis; the general craving for a sure means of success in times of military exigencies and terrible droughts—all these events rendered it possible and profitable for the Mughal sovereigns to store high values in individual denominations. As for the theories of Thomas and Cunningham, Mr. Hodivala assures us in his important work of his authoritative testimony as to their being no longer tenable.*

The attentive ear of the careful hearer of this paper cannot fail to remember that Surat paid its dues in the

* *Op. Cit.*, p. 79.

reign of Akbar in *Muhmudis.* The *Muhmudi* is not a coin issuing out of the imperial mint at the capital or the provincial mints at Surat. It was minted at the Baglana Rajah's mint at Mulhar. Such is the general currency of this coin during the first half of the seventeenth century that the factors of the East India Company at Surat were compelled to send their 'rialls' or Spanish dollars to Mulhar and have them melted down and reminted in *Muhmudis.* It was a generic as well as a popular designation of the silver coins of the Sultans of Guzrae often from very earlier times, and its ratio with tht Akbari rupee stood at 5 : 12, *i.e.*, roughly speaking, two and a half *Muhmudis* went to make a rupee of Akbar.

"The reign of Jehangir marks an epoch in the history of Mughal numismatics and was distinguished by several notable events."* "No reader of Jehangir's 'Memoirs' could fail to have been struck by the pride and satisfaction with which he enlarged upon the rarity, value and beauty of the presents and offerings made to him on the Nauroj, the anniversary of his birth and other court festivals."† A prince noted for hilarity, indifference and fashion, Jehangir designed several innovations in the structure of the coins, the superscriptions that adorn them and the relative values of such denominations.

Of the smaller coins that draw our attention, there are many that were current during his reign. As we have already seen, a special coin the *Nisari* was struck by Jehangir for purposes of *Nisar* or scattering of gold or silver coins and other miniature imitations of fruits and

* Hodivala : *Historical Studies, etc.*, p. 170.

† *Ibid.*, p. 109.

flowers among the people. It is one of the terminological novelties of Jehangir and its actual weight did not matter. There is no necessity to maintain a constancy in its value, since the size, the design and the metal contained in the coin depended always upon the amount of money which the emperor was willing to scatter among his subjects. Hence special orders were to be promulgated as to the mintage of such coin at the pleasure of the emperors, and we can easily connect the date of an imperial stay in a town where a provincial mint was situated and the date when a particular coin intended for the purpose of *Nisar* was minted.

Darbs and *Charns* are other pieces which are to be frequently met with in the statements of Jehangir. They were originally the fanciful designations invented by Akbar to a half and a quarter of the square rupee respectively. Jehangir was so fond of *Darbs* that he commonly states donations to foreign ambassadors in terms of those coins. The probable reason behind it is that Jehangir might have had a notion that foreign travellers would best appreciate and comprehend the real significance of his munificence if the value of the gift was represented in terms of a coin which is almost an equivalent to the highest silver coin in their own country. Thus the *Abbasi*, the highest Persian monetary denomination in silver, is almost equal to the half rupee of Akbar, and the *Darb* is only worth half a rupee. The *Charn*, as already noted, is worth a quarter of a rupee.

Tanki pieces are too frequently met with in the annals of the reign of Jehangir. The pearl and the jewel trades often made use of the *Tank* as a common weight and the *Tanki* was both a weight and a coin like the *Dam Akbar*. It saw its genesis in the creative power of Akbar and it grew into prominence in the reign of Jehangir subject to the modulating influences of local variations, and it was about sixty-four grains troy in weight. " . . . these *Tanki* pieces were struck with a view to provide for the copper currency as complete a series of fractional pieces as existed for the rupee (both square and round)."*

The *Cambray Tankas* and the *zodiacal coins* are other coins of note in the reign of Jehangir, leaving aside for the present moment his so-called " Portrait Muhrs " and heavy coins. We have the emperor's own testimony to the effect that the *Cambray Tankas* of gold and silver minted at Cambray were double the weight of the ordinary *Muhar* and rupee of Akbar. Before Jehangir's reign only *Tankas* of copper were minted and, properly speaking, gold and silver *Tankas* date from his reign.

Perhaps the *zodiacal coins* of Jehangir and of Nurjahan represent a revolutionary innovation made by the emperor. Except for the emperor's own testimony no other historical evidence relating to such coins is to be found. The royal autobiographer goes on to say that a sudden notion which entered his mind makes him decree that the coins should bear the figure of the constellation which belonged to the month in which the coins were struck instead of the normal mint-place. And Tavernier's yarn about Nurjahan dancing before Jehangir, obtaining the promise from him to the effect that she should be

* Hodivala: *Loc.*, p. 113.

installed queen *de facto* for one day, and of the minting of gold and silver coins bearing her own name is more like a folk-tale than an historical exegesis.

Let us now turn to the heavy coins and the so-called *Portrait Muhrs* of Jehangir. There is the emperor's own report that the gold and silver coins minted during his reign were heavier than the ordinary coins of Akbar, and that he gave new names to such coins. Thus the gold coin *Nur-Jahani* and the silver *Sikka-i-Jehangiri* in contradistinction to the *Rupi-i-Jehangiri* besides showing clean traces of nomenclatural innovations were both heavier than the ordinary Akbari *Muhar* and silver rupee by twenty per cent. Both these coins were generally known as *Jehangiris.* Even among these abnormal issues there are two distinct varieties. Being heavier by a fourth and a fifth than the ordinary *Muhar* and rupee of Akbar, they weighed 204 grains and 212½ grains respectively in the case of the gold Muhrs, while the silver coins stood respectively at 214 and 222½ grains. But the standard of fineness of the coins belonging to the previous reign was scrupulously conformed to and hence the coins exchanged in the proportion of their intrinsic weights. Besides these, two distinct types of silver coins were distinguished as *Jehangiris* from the ordinary *Chalani* or *Khajanah* rupees. Even though these abnormal issues were forbidden in the sixth regnal year there were enough coins to be employed in commercial transactions even late in his reign. The minting of the normal Akbari rupees and Muhrs was very rare though not altogether suspended during the first six regnal years. There are a certain number of coins that do not exactly fit into the purport of these statements and the probable conclusion is that they were sporadic issues uncommon as the regular medium of exchange and directly responsible to the ill-trained mint-masters of the provincial mints situated in the outlying districts of the empire.

The fact that the so-called *Portrait Muhrs* were of rare occurrence is apparent from the simple manifestation that the Indian museum can boast of only one of such *Muhrs*, and that another coin is registered in Mr. Whitehead's catalogue. The imperial autobiographer informs us that he specially ordered the mintage of gold pieces weighing one tola with the superscription of the Padisha's effigy on the one side and the figure of Allah surmounted by a sun on the other. These 'Portrait Muhrs' or special medals were only intended for presentation by the emperor to eminent dignitaries of the State as a mark of imperial favour and general distinction, while the emperor took actual pleasure in seeing those medals worn by them with a sort of fetish reverence. "They were, in their origin, only medals or badges of distinction, insignia of an exalted order of Nobility of Merit, or the proofs of the wearer belonging to the inner circle at court."* As for the polemics concerning the superscriptions on the *Portrait Muhr* and their nature and import, it is beyond the scope of this paper, and not profitable from the viewpoint of investigation of this subject. But certain it is that they were presentation tokens ostentatiously indulged in by the emperor, solicitously acquiesced in by the chief persons of the State.

* Hodivala : *Historical Studies, etc.*, p. 149.

The reign of Shah Jehan brings us to view the matter from another side. It is not so much the neologisms and novelties introduced by him as the restoration of the lunar computation of dates that arrests our attention on a close examination of his coins. Students of Mughal history will be aware of the radical innovation by Akbar of the *Ilahi* era based on the solar system of computation beginning with his first regnal year. Jehangir discontinued the *Ilahi* era, but never pretended to have begun a new era of his own. But the official reckoning of the dates by the *Julus* or regnal years was never dispensed with. Jehangir's *Julus* dates come to an end with his death just as he did away with the *Ilahi* era of his father; Shah Jehan went a step further in the direction of orthodoxy by ordering the recounting of years according to the lunar computation. Aurangzib with his great zeal for Muhammadan orthodoxy, abolished the *Naures* celebrations which rung the death-knell of Akbar's anti-Muslim innovations.

The reign of Aurangzib is not specially noteworthy from the numismatic point of view. His reign, as we have already seen, was only remarkable for the great depreciation in the value of silver rendered so by the great influx of silver into India, and for the actual adoption of a silver currency in the empire.

CHAPTER VI.

Conclusion.

If a dispassionate account of the nature of the Mughal Land Revenue System is desired, and if a real appreciation of the system is intended we have to compare the system with those prevailing before and after its existence. Let us now compare the Hindu systems of revenue collection on the one hand, the gradually evolved system of the British administrators of India on the other hand with the rough and ready kind of revenue administration given by the Mughals to their newly conquered empire.

We have already seen that the ideal form of Hindu assessment was the demand by the State of one-sixth of the gross produce of the land. Even farther back, according to Manu, the demand of one-sixth, much less of one-fourth, of the gross produce of the land by the State denotes an exceptionally rare occurrence. Gradually, Manu's ideal was not conformed to. Under Harsha-vardhana the revenue demand was one-sixth. But later on the ideal became degenerated, the collection of revenue became oppressive and the demand of the kings rose to one-half of the gross produce, besides what is known as *quit-rent* was generally taken, and this eventually led to the extinction of many of the village communities. Coming to more synchronistic periods of Hindu and Mughal rule we find the kingdom of Vijayanagar exacting more than the usual rate of assessment. But Nuniz's statement that nine-tenths was taken is not credible.

Wilks states that twenty illegal cesses were prevailing in the reign of Harihara. Payments in kind were prohibited. On the other hand, under Shivaji, the State's share of the produce was fixed at two-fifths, while there was no farming of the revenues.

The systems of land revenue collection under the Mughals we are quite familiar with by now. Akbar took one-third of the gross produce and remitted several vexatious taxes. His system was essentially ryotwar. Later some changes for the worse were introduced and the State's share was raised to one-half and, at times, even more. The system of farming revenues gained currency and the lot of the peasants turned wretched.

A comparison of the Mughal revenue system with that of the British administrators at the present day does not give us a fair comparative judgment. If ever we want to compare the two systems with any degree of fairness, we have to bear in mind that the present system was the product of a gradual process of evolution. Whereas the Mughal emperors gave a rough and ready kind of land revenue system to a newly conquered country, of course, with some inherent drawbacks, the British administrators alive to orderly and settled government for centuries in their native country were not able to evolve a perfect system until recently without committing many serious blunders. They were obliged to grope their way back to the old Mughal system during the early period of their rule. The present system underwent the sad experiences of the farming of revenue collection to intermediaries prior to the hurried quinquennial settlement of Warren Hastings during the years 1772 to 1777, and the still worse ordeal of the misconceived policy of Lord Cornwallis' "*Permanent Settlement*". It is not till recently that the Ryotwar settlement of Sir Thomas Munro gained recognition, and the modern system dates from 1885. "The basis of this system is the division of the whole area into fields by a cadastral survey, each field being valued at a fixed rate per acre and the assessment settled thereon. A holding is one or more of such fields or of their recognized sub-divisions. The registered occupant of each field deals directly with the Government, and so long as he pays the assessment he is entitled to hold the land for ever and cannot be ejected by Government..............private improvements involve no addition, either present or future, to the assessment."* Such a state of affairs was brought about by Acts such as the Bengal Tenancy Act of 1885 based on principles of fixity of tenure and judicial rents while giving statutory holding for seven years in the case of Oudh, the Act of 1877 guaranteeing against eviction and enhancement of rent; the Land Alienation Act of 1900 providing that "money-lenders, shop-keepers and professional men cannot buy land from hereditary cultivators or hold such land on mortgage for more than twenty years without the consent of the State" and such like measures.

Thus we have seen the pitfalls which the present Government had experienced before it had attained its goal. But the Mughal sovereigns were not given so many chances for drawing experience from makeshifts. As indicated above, they gave a system of a rough and ready kind suitable to their needs. When comparing

* *Imperial Gazetteer*, 1908, XVI, p. 318.

these systems we should not minimize the influence of the age in which they lived, the level of civilization they attained, the consonance of these systems with other co-existing systems, the circumstances which governed their actions—not to shield the vulnerable points in the system but to really comprehend it.

Such was the nature of Mughal land revenue system as we have just now seen. Bare the system stands with its defects and merits and a comparison of it with other systems eclipses its real nature. No doubt the system was essentially severe, but such a state was warranted by the prevailing circumstances, when it became the serious concern of the sovereign to see the peasants not to wax fat and kick in an age of perturbed and perplexed circumstances. Even then we have benevolent reigns like those of Sher Shah and Akbar. Though the land-tax under British administration was mitigated the Government is drawing freely upon the other resources of the country in the form of several taxes. On the other hand the various benefits conferred by the British Government may be pointed. But even at the present day Sir Basil Blackett is enquiring about the able resources of the country.

On the one hand the income-tax was amended to provide even "for the assessment of income, profits or gains of an association or club which is neither a company nor a firm nor a Hindu undivided family."* The "supplementary demands" of the finance member amounting

* The *Quarterly Register*, edited by H. N. Mitra, Vol. I, No. i, p. 123.

to over a million rupees,* and his quaint confession:

"I have, I am afraid, already taxed the patience of the House as severely *as the Government are accused of taxing the people of India*"† show that even at the present day, in the very words of the finance member, that the Government "*do not want to remit taxation* or give away a part of the provincial contributions this year and then be faced with the necessity of imposing additional taxation next year or the year after."‡ Yet the Hon. Sir Basil Blackett has the good sense to assure us that the Government "certainly hope for progressive reduction in our military expenditure, for progressive improvement in the yield of our existing sources of revenue. We hope too that the Committee on Taxation will be able, in due course, to recommend important improvements in the machinery and scope of our taxation system so that it may be possible for India to raise in taxation an amount equal to what she raises to-day *at less sacrifice to the tax-payer.*"§

* The *Quarterly Register*, edited by H. N. Mitra, Vol. i, pp. 148—151.

† *Ibid.*, p. 167.

‡ *Ibid.*, p. 173.

§ *Ibid.*, p. 175.

INDEX.

B—*Contd.*

C.

D.

E.

F.

G.

H.

I.

K.

L.

M.

S—*Contd.*

T.

T—*Contd.*

V.

W.

Y.

Z.

www.ingramcontent.com/pod-product-compliance
Ingram Content Group UK Ltd.
Pitfield, Milton Keynes, MK11 3LW, UK
UKHW021408190726
13845UKWH00028B/965

9 789366 082066